Unusual Prophecies Being Fulfilled

Book Four

Understanding the Prophetic Seasons We Are In

Unusual Prophecies Being Fulfilled

Book Four

The Pope, the Eagle and the Iron Sickle

Perry Stone, Jr.

All Scripture is taken from the New King James Version of the Bible, unless otherwise indicated.

ISBN: 0-9785920-2-6

Voice of Evangelism Outreach Ministries
P.O. Box 3595
Cleveland, Tennessee, 37320
(423) 478-3456
Fax: 423-478-1392
www.Perrystone.org

Printed in the United States of America

Contents

Introduction

Once, common citizens throughout Europe were unable to study the Bible. The written Scriptures were not printed for, or available to, the common individual. Only priests or monks in monasteries were favored with copies of the Bible. Eventually, men such as John Wycliff, with threats on their lives, boldly set out to translate the Bible. Such efforts cost many pioneers of Bible translation their lives.

At that season, leaders in the Roman church resisted any attempt to translate and copy the Word of God for the common man. The church felt they were the guardians of Scripture, and only the church hierarchy could correctly interpret them. The biggest challenge of this belief was the 1611 translation of the Bible into the English language. It also impacted the personal views of many within the Roman church.

Today, both Protestants and Catholics (especially in the English-speaking west) actively engage in personal Bible study, especially as it relates to Biblical prophecy. Catholics are discovering the amazing predictions in Revelation 17 and 18, which point to the one-hour destruction of the city of Rome and the Roman church system in the final days.

Both Protestants and Catholics can see in Scripture the emergence of a system that will produce the False Prophet of Revelation 13:11. Many prophetic students are beginning to agree, for the first time, that Rome, Italy, the city of seven hills, will be destroyed in one hour during the final hours of the seven-year Great Tribulation (see Revelation 17).

Many Protestants, however, are unaware of a series of Catholic prophecies concerning the last days and the now-famous predictions from a man named Saint Malachy, concerning the successions of the Popes. Many have never heard of the vision of Our Lady of Fatima and the prediction that Communism would fall. Most have never considered the strange link of three world leaders in the 1980s, whose administrations helped fulfill certain predictions made in 1917.

This book is an amazing story of three world leaders who came to power during the same season of history; and through the direction of Pope John Paul II, helped to fulfill a prediction from 1917. You will see how a defective, apostate Roman leader will eventually unite a branch of Islam and apostate Christianity under his leadership, in the time of the Antichrist. He will fill the position of the False Prophet in Revelation 13.

Let me say at the outset that this book is not designed or intended to debate doctrinal differences between Catholics and Protestants. It is not intended to either authenticate or reject any alleged apparition of Mary we will examine. This is, however, a book that weaves strange events of the past with an understanding of the future. This book will help to unlock a great prophetic mystery, which I believe will enlighten and amaze you!

Sincerely,

Perry Stone, Jr.

Read this Page First

This is Book Four in my series, *Unusual Prophecies Being Fulfilled.* Without doubt, it is one of the most unique of the series. The prophetic insights in this book are not commonly taught, and will be introduced for the first time to many readers.

My only request is that you read the ***entire book*** before you form an opinion or make a final judgment concerning this unique prophetic concept.

I deal extensively with certain prophetic beliefs among those of the Catholic faith, and explore the alleged apparitions of Mary—especially the 1917 apparition in Fatima, Portugal.

Again, it is not my intention to debate Protestant or Catholic doctrine nor try to authenticate or reject any alleged apparition. My purpose is to reveal an amazing series of events that initiated the fall of the Iron Curtain. I will show the unusual link between this event and possible future prophetic events in the Book of Revelation.

This book reveals the link that connects the future Antichrist and False Prophet to their control of Jerusalem for 42 months. It shows how a final religion and the miracle of a talking image will deceive much of the world into following this dynamic duo of the abyss.

Many prophecy ministers emphasize the rise of the future Antichrist, but seldom if ever mention the "other beast" of Revelation 13:11, the false prophet. They also forget that this false prophet will initiate the infamous Mark of the Beast, predicted in Revelation 13:16-18.

I will also include in this book how the conspiracy theory called the Da Vinci Code, is re-introducing goddess worship to the world, and how this rebirth of an ancient religion will also come into play in the final days. All in all, this will be the most unique and stirring book of our series thus far.

For thus says the Lord: After seventy years are completed at Babylon, I will visit you and perform My good word toward you, and cause you to return to this place (Jeremiah 29:10).

1

The 70 Years of the Iron Empire

For over 70 years the iron fist of Communism gripped millions of souls in a cold, atheistic vise, until the rise of three world leaders whom Divine Providence would use to help melt the iron curtain and bring about an unexpected and surprising freedom with a form of democracy. This occurred to many nations previously ruled by Communism.

Western nations could never have imagined, at the turn of the 20th century, the numerous events with prophetic implications that would unfold on the global stage. Just as the script of a play is enacted a chapter at a time, World War I in 1914 was Act One. This was followed in 1941 by Act Two, World War II.

Both wars, along with several smaller wars, kept mapmakers busy redrawing borders. They displaced millions of refugees and caused death to millions of innocent people. These wars would help unfold an unexpected pattern of Bible prophecy. This pattern would turn aligned nations into dangerous enemies.

After World War I, the Russian revolution of 1917 gave birth to the Communist Party in the former Russian Empire. The communist doctrine, as penned and expounded by Karl Marx was espoused by other revolutionaries, and communism eventually spread like a cancer through former Russia and created the Soviet Union, whose national emblem was the hammer and the sickle.

The relentless expansion of communism eventually erected an "iron curtain" across Eastern Europe, and a new system that held its population within its borders and restrained Westerners from entering.

The Rise of Russia

The new union of Soviet states canceled the freedom to express religious beliefs, controlled its population through government intervention, and would not allow disgruntled citizens to receive visas to travel to the West.

Communist doctrine forced religious faith out of the lives of the people in many nations with rich heritages and filled with historic churches. Atheism was Communism's official belief system. Soon after the communists gained control of power in Russia, churches were closed, Bibles were confiscated and countless ministers were arrested.

Children were forced to study the Communist doctrine from an early age, and soon the persecution against Christians had cost the lives of hundreds of thousands of believers. No one dared speak of God or personal faith in public, and the true Christian church went underground. If this was not enough, within 20 years another “ism” arose in Germany.

Under the leadership of the German Chancellor, Adolph Hitler, an evil called Fascism, or Nazism, began to compete with Communism for the control of men, women and children throughout much of Europe. Eventually World War II erupted and pitted Communism against Nazism.

From 1939 to 1945, seven years of destruction and death tore Europe apart. More than six million Jews were exterminated in Nazi gas chambers, ovens and death camps.

70 Years of Captivity

Finally, the war ended, and the continent of Europe was divided between Communism and Democracy. The nation of Germany was divided between East Germany and West Germany as the communists were rewarded half of the country for their involvement in the war.

For 70 years—from 1917 to 1987—the Iron Curtain held millions of souls in spiritual captivity. Suddenly and without warning, one chapter of history closed and a new chapter was opened. Three world leaders set out with the same agenda—to challenge and change the Communist stronghold in Eastern Europe and the Soviet Union.

Two of the men had personal prophecies from the Holy Spirit spoken over them many years before they took public office; and two of the men experienced an assassination attempt that would change their life's purpose and destiny.

These three men were Ronald Reagan, Mikhail Gorbachev and Pope John Paul II.

> ***John Paul II*** *was chosen by the College of Cardinals as Pope of the Roman Catholic Church on October 16, 1978.*
>
> ***Ronald Reagan*** *was elected the 40th President of the United States in 1980.*
>
> ***Mikhail Gorbachev*** *became the head of the Soviet Union in 1985.*

These three world leaders formed a prophetic trio of influence that I call the Pope, the Eagle and the Iron Sickle. These three men helped change the course of history and the future of Communism in what was one of the greatest prophetic events to occur in the 20th century.

This change also initiated a new direction for the world, a direction which paved a road leading to the last days predicted by the Biblical prophets.

Then I saw another angel flying in the midst of heaven, having the everlasting gospel to preach to those who dwell on the earth—to every nation, tribe, tongue, and people (Revelation 14:6).

2

The Pope, the Eagle and the Iron Sickle

These three men, Ronald Reagan, Mikhail Gorbachev and Karol Jozef Wojtyla (Pope John Paul II), will go down as legends in world history for being the trio which, behind the scenes, helped to bring about the greatest political changes in modern history. I refer to the collapse and demise of Communism in the Soviet Union and the Eastern bloc of Europe.

Few Americans are aware of a personal prophecy given to Ronald Reagan while he was governor of California. The prophecy revealed his future destiny as President of the United States.

According to the book, *Reagan Inside Out*, the story begins in California on a beautiful October day in 1970.

Herbert E. Ellingwood, Governor Reagan's legal affairs secretary, had invited several guests to visit the Governor. Among them was celebrity Pat Boone, Harold Bredesen and a minister named George Otis. Boone was a longtime friend of the Reagans, and the Governor at that time was running for re-election.

According to those present that day, the conversations included a discussion on Bible prophecy and the move of the Holy Spirit in the "last days." After a remarkable session of interesting discussion, Ellingwood led the group toward the front door and the final goodbyes were being said.

One of the ministers spoke up and asked, "Governor, do you mind if we take a moment and pray for you and Mrs. Reagan?" Immediately, Reagan replied, "We would appreciate that," as his countenance turned rather serious.

Then the group joined hands, forming a circle. Reagan bowed his head rather sharply and the others tilted theirs a bit. Prayer was immediately offered, asking for God's blessings. Suddenly, in the middle of the prayer, the unexpected occurred. George Otis recalled what transpired:

> *The Holy Spirit came upon me and I knew it. In fact, I was embarrassed. There was this pulsing in my arm, and my hand—the one holding Governor Reagan's hand—was shaking. I didn't know what to do. I just didn't want this to be happening. I can remember, even as I was speaking, tensing my muscles, trying to get the shaking to stop.*

As this was transpiring, the prayer of Otis changed completely, from the basic prayer of blessing to a more steady and intent word. The Holy Spirit-inspired words coming from Otis's mouth spoke directly to Reagan, addressing him as "My Son." The words that came forth recognized his role as leader in a state that was the size of many nations on earth. His "labor" was described as "pleasing." Suddenly the following words were spoken:

> *If you walk uprightly before me, you will reside at 1600 Pennsylvania Avenue.*

Everyone knew that 1600 Pennsylvania Avenue is the address of the White House, the home of America's Presidents.

Ten years passed and in 1980, Governor Reagan, against all odds, ran for President. Ten other Republican candidates were seeking their party's nomination, and he was on the bottom of the pile. The major factor against him was his age; for as he neared the time of the election, he was approaching his 70th birthday.

Political analysts were critical, saying he was "too old to make a correct decision, and he could die while in office." Others said he was incompetent and just an actor. Despite all of the objections, Reagan won. He was then re-elected for a second term. He not only lived to be 78, but past the age of 90!

In November 1980, upon hearing that Reagan had been elected, Pat Boone telephoned the Reagans at their Pacific Palisades home to congratulate Ronald. He first spoke with Nancy, then Reagan came to the phone.

During the conversation, Boone inquired if Reagan remembered the prayer in Sacramento 10 years earlier. Reagan said, "Of course I do."

Ten years before his election as President, God revealed His will for Ronald Reagan. Mr. Reagan was a dedicated Christian and loved the Bible. He was familiar with Biblical prophecy, and at times privately consulted key ministers to ask for input on how certain world events would play into the prophetic scenarios of Scripture.

On the opposite side of the globe, behind the Iron Curtain of the Soviet Union, another divine "setup" was unfolding in the very stronghold of communism.

The Russian Prophecy of 1855

Sixty-two years before the rule of Communism, a man named Dr. Hudson Taylor was ministering. It was written of Taylor, a missionary to China, "For forty years the sun never rose on China, but that Hudson Taylor was on his knees praying for the salvation of the Chinese."

In 1855, during one of his furloughs to England, Taylor was preaching when suddenly he stopped. He stood speechless for a time with his eyes closed. When he began to speak he explained:

> *I have just seen a vision. I saw in this vision a great war that will encompass the whole world. I saw this war recess and then start again, actually being two wars. After this, I saw much unrest and revolts that will affect many nations. I saw in some places, spiritual awakenings.*
>
> *In Russia, I saw there will come a general, all-encompassing spiritual awakening so great that there could never be another like it. From Russia, I saw the awakening spread to many European countries. Then I saw an all-out awakening followed by the coming of Christ.* (From an original article, "Spiritual Revival," published in Finland in 1945.)

Sixty-two years after Hudson's vision, the Russian Revolution adopted Communism. This anti-God system grew like a poison vine, choking to death individual faith in God. For 70 years, the sword of godless Communism dripped with the blood of Christian martyrs and Communist resisters. The West never comprehended the possibility that the Iron Curtain would fall and religious freedom would rise like steam from hot water.

Since a true communist must be a confessed atheist, Western Christians reasoned it was impossible for the oppressed Soviet Christians to ever see the chains of oppression fall off. Yet, a few underground believers in the unregistered Pentecostal church were aware of a prophecy given in the 1930s, revealing that one day religious freedom would come!

This prophetic word was guarded and cherished by leaders in the church there for over 50 years. Several years ago, the old prophecy was told directly to the Reverend Lovell R. Carey, former World Missions director for the Church of God, Cleveland, Tennessee, while he was visiting Russia.

1930 Prophecy Concerning Mikhail

Lovell was in Russia shortly after the fall of Communism. He met with one of the bishops of the unregistered Pentecostal church, Bishop Fedatov.

According to the bishop, in the 1930s a Christian woman gave an unusual prophetic word under the inspiration of the Holy Spirit. It said in the future a person would arise in the Soviet Union whose name would be Mikhail. He would have a mark on his forehead.

She continued her prophecy, saying that during his time there would once again be freedom to worship and revival would come to the nation. This freedom would be only for a short time, however; then repression would begin again.

Fifty years later, the prophecy was fulfilled—Mikhail Gorbachev became leader of the Soviet Union! *Glasnost* became a global word. A lesser known part of the story concerning Mr. Gorbachev, however, reveals the timing of the Almighty's hand in raising up men to rule.

A Christian Mother Influences Mikhail

Lavon Riley was a tour operator from Texas. In the late 1980s, Mr. Riley planned a trip to Russia, traveling with a group of Christians. Their plane carried thousands of Bibles. Upon their arrival, it was difficult to get clearance for the Bibles; but after a detailed visit with customs personnel and a special permit, the army came with trucks and delivered the Bibles directly to the churches.

Lavon told this author personally, that the KGB called him into their offices during this trip. He was in great fear of being arrested. The personnel of the KGB proceeded to tell him they were aware of his every step. "In fact," the man in charge said, "Let me show you your file." He pulled out a file about four inches thick, that gave details of every time Lavon had ever traveled to Russia, including places he had spoken, the hotels he had stayed in and the restaurants where he had eaten.

It turned out the meeting was not to arrest or interrogate him, but to demonstrate to him that a "New Russia" existed, that would permit more religious freedom. A permit was given to Lavon, by the third man under Gorbachev, to bring as many Bibles into Russia as Lavon desired!

During this time Lavon learned that the mother of Mikhail Gorbachev was an Orthodox Christian. She had prayed for Mikhail for many years, that he would become a leader in Russia. He also learned that for Mikhail's birthday, his mother would make a special cake and place certain Scriptures on it.

This was confirmed when Gorbachev appeared on the Hour of Power with Robert Schuller on October 22,

2000. He spoke about his mother's prayers and said that "practically all" of his family was Christian. During the interview Mikhail said, "There can be no freedom without spiritual freedom, without human beings being able to choose."

While Mikhail has kept close ties to the Russian Orthodox Church, no one can deny that *perestroika* created an atmosphere of coexistence, opening the door to freedom of religious expression without repression. Apparently, the predestined purpose of Gorbachev was two-fold:

- ❑ *to bring religious freedom to the Soviet Union (Russia), and*
- ❑ *to allow the Soviet Jews to return to Israel.*

This action was also a direct fulfillment of ancient Biblical prophecies concerning the return of the Jews from the North Country to Israel. In the Bible, Israel was in captivity in Babylon for exactly 70 years (Jeremiah 25:11). God gave Israel the Ten Commandments and warned them that if they disobeyed Him, the punishment would be seven times (Leviticus 26:18). Ten multiplied seven times totals the number 70.

In 1917, Communism took its hold in Russia and for seventy years held people captive. Seventy years later, in 1987, the breakdown of the Iron Curtain began. While visiting Germany, President Reagan demanded that Gorbachev tear down the Berlin Wall dividing Germany. Later Mr. Gorbachev not only allowed the Wall to be demolished, but helped to unbolt the mighty iron curtain over Russia and Eastern Europe. Both men rose to power at a pivotal season in history.

Daniel tells us God "changes the times and the seasons; He removes kings and raises up kings" (Daniel 2:21). As the hand of Providence was moving "pawns" into position on His chess board, one more important move was needed to put Communism into "checkmate!"

The "Prophetic" Role of Karol Wojtyla

On May 18, 1920, Karol Jozef Wojtyla was born in Wadowice, Poland. During the Nazi occupation of Poland, Karol pursued his studies. He worked as a stonecutter to hold a work permit, thus keeping him from being deported or imprisoned. He joined the UNIA, a Christian democratic underground group. Jewish organizations, such as B'nai B'rith, testified that he helped Jews find refuge from the Nazis.

In 1942 he began studying for the priesthood, and was ordained a priest on November 1, 1946. By 1967 he was elevated to cardinal and on October 16, 1978, at age 58, Karol Wojtyla was elected Pope and chose the title of John Paul II.

Two Assassination Attempts

Oddly, both Reagan and the Pope survived assassination attempts on their lives in the same year!

On May 13, 1981, the Pope greeted a crowd at Vatican Square in Rome, Italy. As he leaned over to kiss a statue of the Virgin Mary, a Turkish terrorist fired a gun, and the Pope was struck in the abdomen by the assassin's bullet. He slumped into the arms of his secretary as blood poured from the wound. The world prayed and waited, concerned that the Pope would die.

Despite losing six pints of blood, John Paul II survived. The Pope realized he had been shot on the 64-year anniversary of the famous Marion apparition known as Our Lady of Fatima.

This alleged apparition of the Virgin Mary is said to have appeared to three children in Fatima, Portugal on May 13, 1917 (the same year of the Communist revolution in Russia). Because of this strange coincidence, the Pope credited "Our Lady of Fatima" (the Virgin Mary) with sparing his life, and dedicated the remaining time of his papacy to her "immaculate heart."

It was also 1981 when President Reagan spoke at a luncheon at the Hilton Hotel in Washington, D.C. As he exited a side door, waving at reporters, a young man named John Hinckley fired six shots at the president. As secret service agent Jerry Parr hit Reagan in the stomach (to double him over into the limousine), both men realized the president had been shot.

A single bullet ricocheted off the limo door and entered Reagan's chest. X-rays at the hospital revealed the assassin's bullet had stopped just an inch from Reagan's heart! In *An American Life: The*

Autobiography, Reagan said: "I remember looking up from the gurney, trying to focus my eyes on the ceiling tiles, and praying."

In the emergency room, the President realized someone was holding his hand. The hand touched his, holding on tight. He remembers a comforting, reassuring feeling. He asked several times who was holding his hand, but received no response. He later tried to find out who held his hand, assuming it was a nurse. He was never able to locate the "person." Reagan confessed, "Someone was looking out for us on that day." Reagan told several Secret Service agents he gave credit to God for protecting his life.

These two assassination attempts helped bond a special relationship between the President and the Pope. In June, 1982, Ronald Reagan flew to the Vatican for a personal meeting with Pope John Paul II. Years later, their private discussion was made public. Both men discussed their assassination attempts, and agreed that God had spared their lives for a specific reason.

As they continued their discussion, they began to see a common thread of destiny. Both men discussed the terrible scourge of communism, and how the oppressive regimes had destroyed personal freedoms and faith in God for millions of people who desired to be delivered from the iron hold of this anti-God system.

At that moment, both men pledged to work together to help spread freedom throughout Communist nations. The Pope knew all too well about communism, since his homeland of Poland was a nation gripped in the Communist vice.

Reagan did more than talk of freedom. Three weeks after the meeting, he signed a secret National Security Directive to purchase and send to Poland the necessary equipment—including copy machines, fax machines and other electronic equipment—to assist the Solidarity Movement working in Poland. This group would organize protests that would be aired via satellite around the world and would unite a large following of Polish workers.

The plan worked. Just as the idea of communism had captured the minds of the common people during the 1917 revolution, it was the common workers of Poland who took the keys of freedom and unshackled the bands of iron.

The impact of their uprising soon spread to Romania, Bulgaria and East Germany, where the world was stunned as the famous Berlin Wall was dismantled by the German people! Before Reagan departed from office, the Berlin Wall had crumbled, the Soviet Union had unraveled and the icy Cold War had melted.

A report in *Time* magazine stated (February 24, 1992) that the coalition between Reagan and the Vatican consisted of a five-part strategy "aimed at bringing about the collapse of the Soviet economy, fraying the ties that bound the USSR to its client states in the Warsaw Pact, and forcing reform inside the Soviet empire."

Both Reagan and Gorbachev admitted the vital role the Pope played in the collapse of Communism in Eastern

Europe. Few non-Catholics understand one of the unseen motives behind the Pope's decision to become directly involved in liberating the Eastern Block Communist countries, especially the Soviet Union. His spiritual inspiration hinged upon a prophecy given through an alleged apparition of the Virgin Mary in 1917.

The Prophecy of Fatima

Pope John Paul credited the Virgin Mary with sparing his life. One year after his near-death experience, the Pope traveled to a famous Catholic shrine in Fatima, Portugal. He presented one of the bullets used in the attack on his life, and asked that it be placed in the crown of the statue of "Our Lady of Fatima" as a token of gratitude for her saving his life.

The Pope pledged himself to Mary, and gave himself to her message, especially the message of Fatima. His personal motto was *Totus Tuus Sum Maria*, meaning, "Mary, I am all yours." On May 13, 1982, the Pope prayed before the statue of our Lady of Fatima and consecrated the world to her, based on the promise from 1917. That promise said, "If my wishes are fulfilled . . . my immaculate heart will triumph, Russia will be converted and there will be peace."

From that moment it was the goal of the Pope to see Communism fall in the Eastern Bloc countries of Europe, including the Soviet Union. The Pope would receive help from the Eagle of America (Reagan) and from a leader living under the Iron Sickle, Mikhail Gorbachev.

As are most traditional European Catholics, the Pope was very much aware of the prophecies given in Fatima, Portugal, in 1917, concerning the future fall of Communism. Because the Pope's life was spared on the anniversary of the Fatima visitation, he was compelled in his spirit to help fulfill the "wishes of the Virgin Mary" proclaimed at Fatima, that Russia would be converted.

Let's look at these prophecies.

I will stand my watch . . . to see what He will say to me. . . . Then the Lord answered me and said: "Write the vision and make it plain . . . that he may run who reads it" (Habakkuk 2:1, 2).

3

The 1917 Prophecies from Fatima

The name *Fatima* is known to most Catholics, but unknown to most Protestants. The name alludes to an alleged visitation of the Virgin Mary to the village of Fatima, Portugal, in 1917.

The Moors once occupied Portugal, and the village of Fatima was named after a princess of the nearby Castle of Ourem. At birth, the princess was named Fatima, like many Muslim girls, in honor of the daughter of Muhammad. (He said that Fatima, his daughter, had the highest place in heaven after the Virgin Mary.) The princess married the Count of Ourem and converted to Christianity.

In 1910, a revolution in Portugal initiated a separation of church and state. The ruling class was anti-religious and had dissolved religious congregations and confiscated church property. News articles called religion mere superstition and mocked any form of religious ritual. Despite this transition, among the poor in the rural areas religion was still considered a part of daily life. An event that began in 1916 would eventually mark Portugal for decades to come.

Just 88 miles north of Lisbon lies the tiny village of Fatima. According to Jewish tradition, Ishmael, Abraham's son, married a woman named Fatima. She was chosen by his mother, Hagar, from among the Egyptians (Genesis 21:21). Centuries later, the founder of Islam had six children—five sons and a girl named Fatima.

Fatima married Ali to carry on the descendants of Muhammad. She gave birth to two sons, Hassan and Hussein. Shiite Muslims claim their right to be the true branch of Islam because their early caliphs were from Ali and Fatima's lineage.

The Visions of Fatima

In 1916, reports began circulating in the village of Fatima, Portugal, that an angel had appeared to a seven-year-old girl named Lucia dos Santos. The first manifestation materialized over the tops of trees on the side of a hill. This apparition told the girl, "Jesus and Mary have merciful designs on you."

Later, the same angel appeared again to Lucia and her two younger cousins, Francisco and Jacinta Marto, between May 13 and October 13, 1917. The children claim that the angel, after speaking to them, held a chalice with his left hand. A host (wafer) above the chalice dripped blood into the cup.

On May 13, 1917 the three children, ages six, eight and nine, were playing together in a field called Cova da Iria. It was noon and they were shepherding sheep. Suddenly a spring rain began falling. Since it was accompanied by lightning, the children took refuge in a nearby cave.

As they waited for the rain to pass, they said that suddenly something appeared in front of them that looked like a white globe moving. They claimed to have seen a "person" clothed in light who said he was an angel of peace. He told the three children, "Pray . . . the hearts of Jesus and Mary have merciful designs for you. Offer prayers and sacrifices continuously."

Later, in the fall of the same year, the children described seeing a golden cup and a host. They reported they saw blood dripping in the cup that was suspended in midair. These words were heard:

> *Sacrifice yourselves for sinners, and repeat often . . . . "O Jesus, it is for love of You and the immaculate heart of Mary, I beg thee for the conversion of poor sinners."*

These words were also allegedly heard: "I want you to come here at this same hour on the 13th day of each month until October. Then I will tell you who I am and what I want." She told them to "pray the rosary every day and bear the suffering God would send."

In June, the children said the apparition appeared again. About 70 percent of the village was present on this occasion, but the children were the only ones who claimed to see the apparition. The apparition predicted that two of the children would leave and go to heaven, and that Lucia would stay.

On July 13 of the same year, the alleged apparition appeared to the three children and revealed a secret message in three parts. For many years people wondered what the messages were. In 1941, Lucia wrote her memoirs and released two parts of the message. The first was a vision of hell. Lucia wrote:

> *Our Lady showed us a great sea of fire which seemed to be under the earth. Plunged in this fire were demons and souls in human form, like transparent burning embers, all blackened or burnished bronze, floating about in the conflagration, now raised into the air by the flames that issued from within themselves together with great clouds of smoke, now falling back on every side like sparks in a huge fire, without weight or equilibrium, and amid shrieks and groans of pain and despair, which horrified us and made us tremble with fear.*
>
> *The demons could be distinguished by their terrifying and repulsive likeness to frightful and unknown animals, all black and transparent. This vision lasted but an instant.*

Lucia continued her prophecy by predicting that "when you see a night illumined by an unknown light, know that this is the great sign given you by God that He is about to punish the world for its crimes, by means of war, famine, and persecutions of the church."

A mere 21 years later, on January 25, 1938, the famous aurora borealis (northern lights) was visible all across Europe—exactly one year before World War II began!

The second "secret" involved the conversion of Russia. The children claim the apparition said:

> *If my requests are heeded, Russia will be converted, and there will be peace; if not, she will spread her errors throughout the world, causing wars and persecutions of the Church. The good will be martyred; the Holy Father will have much to suffer; various nations will be annihilated. In the end, my immaculate heart will triumph. The Holy Father will consecrate Russia to me, and she shall be converted, and a period of peace will be granted to the world.*

Lucia wrote that the apparition then said:

> *In the end my immaculate heart will triumph. The Holy Father will consecrate Russia to me, and she will be converted, and a period of peace will be granted to the world. In Portugal, the dogma of the faith will be preserved.*

The1917 Russian Revolution birthed Communism and an atheistic state throughout the once-strongly religious regions of Russia. It has been reported that millions of Catholic peasants were killed by Stalin, either in the Gulag or by the firing squad, in an attempt to snuff out the Christian faith and demonstrate to other believers that the same fate would follow them if they professed Christianity.

Lucia kept the third secret for 83 years. On May 13, 2000, the pope went to Fatima to beatify Jacinta and Francisco as "Blessed of Heaven." Lucia was present. After the assassination attempt on the Pope in 1981, he was given the third secret, but chose not to reveal it at that time. Subsequently, Pope John Paul II released the much-talked-about third secret.

The Third Secret

The third secret was written down by Lucia and given to Portugal's Bishop of Leiria of Portugal, with instructions not to open the sealed envelope until 1960. In 1957, the Bishop turned the envelope over to the Vatican. It is alleged that Pope John XXIII opened the envelope, but was so stunned by its contents that he refused to discuss them.

John Paul II also read the letter and refused to reveal the contents publicly, saying its "true spiritual message has been obscured by sensationalism." It is said that three popes read the letter, and refused to comment on the vision. In a speech in 1984, the Bishop of Leiria-Fatima spoke in Vienna and stated: "The third secret of Fatima speaks not about atomic bombs, nor about nuclear warheads, nor about SS-20 missiles. Its contents concern but our faith."

On May 13, 2000, the anniversary of the Fatima apparitions and the assassination attempt on Pope John Paul II, the Pope and Lucia met to discuss the third secret, which the Vatican described as a vision of the 1981 assassination attempt on Pope John Paul II. The third secret that Lucia committed to paper on January 3, 1944, allegedly said:

> *The Holy Father passed through a big city half in ruins and trembling with halting step, afflicted with pain and sorrow, he prayed for the souls of the corpses he met on his way; having reached the top of the mountain, on his knees at the foot of the big Cross he was killed by a group of soldiers who fired bullets and arrows at him, and in the same way there died one after another the Bishops, Priests, religious men and women, and various lay people of different ranks and positions.*
>
> *Beneath the arms of the Cross were two angels, each with a crystal aspersorium in his hand, in which he gathered the blood of the Martyrs and sprinkled it on the souls making their way to God.*

Oddly, it was reported in 1996 that the only living person to have seen the entire third secret in detail was Cardinal Joseph Ratzinger, who was head of the Vatican's Congregation for the Doctrine of the Faith. Today, he is Pope Benedict, head of the Catholic Church!

Vatican City, June 26, 2000

Catholic leaders, such as Ratzinger, have pointed out that there is nothing worrisome about the third vision, and the Vatican kept it a secret to avoid "confusing religious prophecy with sensationalism." There are many, however, in the Catholic Church who believe the third vision is more than a prediction of the assassination attempt of John Paul II. Some believe the vision is a detailed account of how the "real pope" will battle the forces of the Antichrist at the time of the end.

Other Catholics, many who share our prophetic views, believe it is an apocalyptic vision linked to the final conflict between the Roman Church and the forces of the Antichrist. Revelation 17 and 18 reveal that the armies of the Antichrist will march into Rome and destroy the city with fire.

The Fatima prediction that Russia would be converted to Christianity if the country would be dedicated to Mary, inspired John Paul II to dedicate Russia to the heart of Mary. So in 1984, the Pope completed his dedication of the world, including the Eastern Bloc and Russia, to "Mary's Immaculate Heart."

This declaration inspired the Pope to travel to Communist countries, drawing huge crowds of the faithful and planting seeds of freedom in the hearts of the multitudes.

This expectation was fulfilled in 1989. Not only did the chains of Communism drop in the Eastern Bloc nations and Russia, but this new freedom allowed Russian Jews to gain visas and return to their ancient homeland of Israel. The Pope's attempted assassination, the link to Fatima, and the 1917 Russian prophecies actually forged a prophetic season in which the prediction could be fulfilled. The Pope understood the predictions, perceived the circumstances and seized the opportunity, using the poverty and discontent created by Communism.

The human desire for spiritual freedom and inner peace connected with the Pope's message in Eastern Europe. Communism could not withstand the fire of freedom burning in the bosoms of men and women. The fact that Ronald Reagan and Mikhail Gorbachev had similar goals—for a new freedom and openness to forge between the East and the West—only added more fuel to the fires of freedom sweeping like a windstorm from nation to nation.

The goals of these three men of prophecy dovetailed into prophetic fulfillment. By the time of Reagan's departure as President and Gorbachev's final year as Russia's leader, Communism as we knew it no longer dominated Eastern Europe or Russia.

Yes, there is still repression in areas. Yes, there will be future conflict. But Russia experienced, during the decade of the 1990s, the great revival visualized by Hudson Taylor.

During this decade, evangelists and religious organizations from the Western nations poured into the former Soviet Union, distributing millions of Bibles as predicted by Biblical prophets. As time passes, so does the leadership of nations and religions. A major change came to the Catholic Church with the death of

Pope John Paul II. Another series of prophecies related to the future of the Catholic Church and the rise of the Biblical Antichrist was resurrected from Vatican archives. These unusual predictions renewed interest in the number of popes that remain until the alleged appearance of the future Antichrist.

These predictions are recognized as the "Prophecies of Saint Malachy," or, "The Prophecy of the Succession of the Popes."

Note: *In writing about this apparition, I am reporting the information as it was alleged to have occurred, to show the motivation that prompted Pope John II to set out to free people from Communism.*

There is a God in heaven who reveals secrets, and He has made known . . . what will be in the latter days (Daniel 2:28).

4

The Prophecies of Saint Malachy

Malachy was born in Northern Ireland in A.D. 1094, ordained a priest in 1119, and was known as a student of the Scriptures. Eventually, he was appointed the Archbishop of Armaga in 1132. According to those personally acquainted with him, he was said to have received the gift of prophecy and witnessed many miracles through his personal prayers. He is even said to have predicted the day and hour of his death.

His most famous predictions are of the future succession of the popes. In 1139, he went to Rome to give an account of his diocese to Pope Innocent II. Historians say that at this time he was given a strange vision of the future, in which he revealed a long list of popes who would rule the church until the end of time. In 1140, Malachy gave the written document to Pope Innocent II to console him in the midst of his tribulations.

It is said that the document remained in the Vatican Archives, unknown, until it was discovered in 1590. The predictions were first printed by the Benedictine historian, Arnold Wion. During the past several hundred years, these predictions seem to surface each time a pope dies and another is appointed to take his place. The prophecies, however, are not without controversy.

The Controversy

Because of the original 400 years of silence on the subject (1139 to 1590), some have suggested that the prophecies were actually forgeries written by a group of Jesuits sometime during the 1600s. This is because the predictions give very clear mottos for all of the future popes up to that period of time.

Historical records show, however, that the prophecies were published in 1559. Yet, the *Catholic Encyclopedia, 1913 Edition,* says about Malachy's prophecies:

> *These short prophetical announcements . . . indicate some noticeable trait of all future popes from Celestine II, who was elected in the year 1130, until the end of the world. They are enunciated under mystical titles. Those who have undertaken to interpret and explain these symbolical prophecies*

> *have succeeded in discovering some trait, allusion, point, or similitude in their application to the individual popes, either as to their country, their name, their coat of arms or insignia, their birthplace, their talent or learning, the title of their cardinalate, the dignities which they held.*
>
> *There is something more than coincidence in the designations given to . . . popes so many hundreds of years before their time. We need not have recourse either to the family names, armorial bearings or cardinalatial titles, to see the fitness of their designations as given in the prophecies.*

Those who follow the order of the predictions discover some trait, some allusion or similitude to each pontiff's coat of arms, birthplace, name, learning, background and so forth. In other words, each prediction gives a clue indicating something about the succession of popes.

Popes in the Past 100 Years

Below is a list of the popes during the past 100 years, and the theme, motto or prediction recorded in the Malachy papers. Each theme is linked to a pope's rule over the Roman Catholic church. In the Malachy predictions, **Pope Benedict XV** (1914-1922), was given the title, *Religion Laid Waste.*

When elected pope in 1914, this man made an attempt to bring peace during World War I, but failed. During his reign, millions of Christians died in World War I. He witnessed the rise of atheistic Communism that brought an end to Christian influence in Russia. This pope saw religion treaded underfoot during his rule.

Pope Pius XI (1922-1939) was given the title, *Unshaken Faith.* His name was Achille Ratti, and he was elected in 1922. During his rule, he faced the spread of Communism and the rise of Nazi Germany. An outspoken critic of Communism and Fascism, he was under extreme pressure from Mussolini, the Italian dictator and fascist.

He ruled in a time when many Christians throughout Europe were experiencing trials and persecution. He died just before the seven-year Holocaust that cost the lives of six million Jews in Germany and Austria.

The Malachy predictions designated the next pope the *Angelic Shepherd.* **Pope Pius XII** (1939-1958) was mystical, and it is said that he received many visions. According to news reports at the time, people would kneel when they received telephone calls from him. Amazingly, if these numbers and prophecies about the future popes were written in the 1500s, the writings reveal some strange and accurate prophetic patterns of the future popes.

Pope John XXIII (1958-1963) was called the *Pastor and Marine.* Prior to his election he was the patriarch of Venice, a marine city. Following John XXIII was **Pope Paul VI** (1963-1978), whose motto Malachy predicted to be *Flower of Flowers.* This prediction was prophetically fulfilled when the College of Cardinals elected as pope a man whose personal coat of arms displayed three lilies.

The year 1978 was a prophetically significant year, and is known as "the year of three Popes." Momentous events of prophecy were fulfilled during this year. The 12 months saw the death of **Pope Paul VI**, the election and death of **Pope John Paul I**, and then the election of **Pope John Paul II.**

The next pope in succession after Paul VI was called *Of the Half of the Moon.* **John Paul I** (1978), lived for only a month after he was elected pope. There was suspicion among some that he was actually poisoned by insiders in the Vatican. He was elected on August 26th and passed away suddenly of unknown causes just one moon cycle later. His body was mysteriously cremated within one day without an autopsy.

Interestingly, John Paul I was elected during a half-moon and died during a half-moon! This pope ruled during a time of conflict with Muslims, whose universal religious emblem is a crescent moon. During his brief rule, Egypt and Israel signed a major peace treaty that led to the historic Camp David Accords.

The next pope elected by the Catholic conclave was Karol Wojityla, who selected the name **John Paul II** (1978-2005). According to the Malachy prediction, he would hold the title of *Of the Eclipse of the Sun,* or *From the Labor of the Sun.*

This pope was born on May 18, 1920, during a solar eclipse. He was buried in Rome on Friday April 8, 2005, in Rome. Strangely, this was during an unusual, major solar eclipse that astronomers call a "hybrid eclipse," because it was both a total eclipse and an annular eclipse.

John Paul II was also involved in helping the Solidarity Movement in Poland, a union of common laborers, in rising up and resisting the Communist's control of the government. These strange predictions, or as some say "coincidences," naturally fuel interest in the remaining predictions made by Malachy.

The Final Pope(s)

According to Vatican historians, John Paul II was the 110th pope from Malachy's day. There seems to be a slight controversy at this point concerning the remaining portion of Malachy's predictions. Some sources indicate that the original prediction had only one more pope listed, Number 111. Others contend that two more popes remain.

In the time of the 112th pope, they say, the city of Rome will be destroyed. Some allege that the prediction of the 112th and final pope was added at a later time. If we use the contemporary list, two popes are to follow Pope John Paul II.

The next pope (the 111th from Malachy's time) was identified with the phrase, *"The Glory of the Olive."* Before the election of Joseph Ratzinger as **Pope Benedict XVI**, there was much speculation stirring as to what this motto actually meant. Some believed the next pope would have a Jewish background, because the *olive tree* is a symbol of Israel and the Jewish people. Others speculated that the pope would be dark complected, or olive skinned, perhaps from Latin America or Africa. Still others suggested he would simply be heavily involved in the peace process, attempting to bring Jews, Christians and Muslims to the peace table.

The Benedictine Order and the 111th Pope

For years, the order of Saint Benedict had predicted the 111th pope would come from their Order and would lead a fight against evil in the world. Before he became Pope, Ratzinger himself prophesied that before the end of the world his Order, known as the Olivetans, would triumphantly lead the Catholic church in its final fight with evil.

Saint Benedict had an interesting history. He was born near Spoleto, Italy, around A.D. 480, during the waning years of the Roman Empire. When he was in his late teens, he traveled with a nurse to Rome to complete his studies in rhetoric and law. According to information written in A.D. 539, Benedict forsook his father's house and wealth to pursue serving God.

Eventually, Benedict chose the life of a hermit and became what we would call a monk. As time progressed, he became well known throughout the surrounding area. He built monasteries and initiated what is called the Benedict Rule. Perhaps the most interesting aspect of Benedict is a prophecy he gave. *It was alleged, according to some Catholic traditions, that he predicted that just before the coming of the Antichrist, a pope will be elected from his order.*

Pope Benedict XVI (2005-)

Why did Joseph Ratzinger, a German cardinal who was elected Pope on April 19, 2005, adopt the title, Pope Benedict? Does this name fit into Malachy's prediction for the 111th pope?

The word *benedict* means "blessing," and we get the word "benediction" from it. The Order of the Benedictines are an order that traces their roots to Saint Benedict. They also call themselves, and are known as, "*The Olivetans!*" If we understand the meaning of the name Benedict and the link to the name Olivetans, then one could understand the prophecy of Malachy, and say it means the "Blessing of the Olive."

Traditionally, the olive branch has been associated with peace, but in both the Old and New Testaments it also serves as an emblem for the Jews. Some commentators believe that the prophesied conversion of the Jews will take place during the tenure of Benedict XVI. He is an older pope (78 when elected), and many have suggested he will not live long, in comparison to other popes who were elected at a younger age.

It is interesting that Jesus gave His apocalyptic prophecy about the last days from the Mount of Olives (Matthew 24).

Only time will tell how long this pope will live and what influence he will wield in the world and over the doctrine of the Catholic church. He appears to be taking a strong conservative stand at this point, which is what was expected from this pope.

Who Is the Final Pope?

Before attempting to answer, let me point out that we must never base our understanding of the prophetic on the vision of someone outside of the Bible, even when the individual is a praying, godly person. Our complete prophetic understanding must come from the revelation of the Biblical prophets.

When a believer has an established reputation of making predictions that continually come to pass, however, then this information should be reviewed and considered as a possible prophetic word in season.

If the succession of the popes is correct, and there will be a 112th pope after Pope Benedict XVI, then what is the prophetic inference linked to the next pope?

According to the more modern interpretation to Malachy's prediction, the final pope will be "Peter the Roman." This in itself seems to be self-explanatory. No pope has ever taken on the name "Peter," since the Roman church adopted the *tradition* of Peter being the first pope.

Calling him the "Roman" implies he will be from Italy or will arise out of the EU or a newly revived Roman Empire. But it is the prediction related to the rise of

Peter the Roman that has caused quite a stir among prophetic Catholics, as well as among those who have followed these predictions.

Many add these final words to Malachy's prediction of the 112th pope in his list of succession:

> *In extreme persecution, the seat of the Holy Roman Church will be occupied by Peter the Roman, who will feed the sheep through many tribulations, after which the City of Seven Hills will be destroyed, and the dreadful Judge will judge the people. The end.*

Another interesting twist develops when some Catholic historians say that Pope John Paul II was a continuation of John Paul I, and the two should be counted as one succession. John Paul I would be the moon half of the prediction, and John Paul II the labor of the sun.

Let me again remind the reader that while these predictions are quite interesting, the final truth of all predictions about the future lies in the prophets and apostles who penned the holy Scriptures. In the Book of Revelation, there is ample evidence of coming events that involve the city of Rome, the Roman church system and the rise of a False Prophet.

Many Catholic and Protestant scholars believe the False Prophet will arise out of the Church of Rome. They believe that toward the end of days, the church will split between those faithful to God and the apostates. It will be the apostates, the compromisers of truth, who will follow the apocalyptic beasts of Revelation 13.

Then I saw another beast coming up out of the earth, and he had two horns like a lamb and spoke like a dragon (Revelation 13:11).

5

The Coming Lamb with Two Horns

Hundreds of thousands of churches and cathedrals are scattered throughout Europe, Russia and the Middle East. Students of world history are aware of the spiritual and political influence of the Church of Rome and the Orthodox churches in that region of the world. As we near the prophetic conclusion of the end of the age, just what role and how much influence will a future pope have among the populace of Europe, and especially the Middle East?

Many Protestant and some Catholic scholars predict a time when an apostate pope will split the Roman church, and Rome itself will be attacked by Islamic fanatics, bringing a fiery conclusion to the long history of the Roman church.

Today, three major religions basically dominate the people groups living throughout Europe, Russia and much of the Middle East. They are the Roman Catholics, the Orthodox Christians and the Muslims. From the initiation of Islam in the 7th century until the present, Catholicism and Islam have experienced seasons of conflict which have erupted from political and religious differences. These have climaxed in wars, conflicts and political tensions throughout Europe and the Middle East.

From time to time, seasons of calm have emerged, only to be broken by another storm of religious conflict.

Muslims often remind Christians of the Crusades, when hundreds of thousands of European Christians thundered into the Middle East to "liberate" the Holy Lands from the control of Muslims. Christians, however, remind Muslims of their more recent invasion at the beginning of the 20th century when over a million Christians were slaughtered in Armenia.

Throughout the 1,400-year history of the Islamic religion, the Roman Church hierarchy has played a major role in appointing kings, initiating invasions and assisting in the support of various wars. Jews remind Christians in the West that Hitler claimed to be a "Christian," and even used Martin Luther's "anti-Semitic" statements to approve the Holocaust.

Through the centuries, Christianity and Islam have seemed worlds apart. In modern times, however, the Church of Rome has been instrumental in negotiating important peace agreements and serving as a sounding board between such groups as Palestinians and Jews, who are divided over the issue of land for peace.

Confusion in the Roman Church

Sex abuse scandals in recent years have caused a major setback to the spiritual and political influence of the Roman church, especially in North America and the West. There are regions of the country in which numerous priests have been arrested and found guilty of sexual abuse among children, especially among young boys who were serving in the church or placing their trust in a spiritual "Father" who failed them.

At first, Rome attempted to say these were isolated cases and not a common pattern. As the truth was revealed by the victims who had been silenced by fear, the scandals have proven to be not only numerous, but financially devastating to the church and emotionally devastating to the faithful.

Will the Roman church survive the future? Presently, countless thousands of Roman Catholics around the world are discovering spiritual fulfillment and refreshment in the Pentecostal-Charismatic Movement, especially in the northeastern United States and in Latin America.

In some nations, Roman churches once filled with worshipers now hold Mass for an older, faithful group, while the younger generation does not attend church. There can be found singing, rejoicing and listening to practical Bible preaching in large mega-churches or independent denominations. Still, multitudes of Catholics remain loyal to the church and the traditions of Rome. What will Rome do to pull in the younger generation?

It may seem strange, but one day there will be a great following of people produced from the merging of two major religions under two leaders—one a military dictator and the other a religious leader.

The universal cry now is for *tolerance.* We are being taught to accept everyone's personal belief, to be tolerant of all religions and to not condemn anyone, even if their religion contradicts the Word of God. This pressure to be tolerant is especially intense among the "seeker sensitive" mega-churches.

They invite people of other religions, such as Hinduism and Buddhism, to take the church's pulpit and "share their faith" among the believers in the church. This kind of emphasis desensitizes people to false doctrine, and will enable a future false prophet to be successful in deceiving the masses with his counterfeit doctrine and miracles.

The Antichrist and the False Prophet

The 13th chapter of Revelation begins unfolding during the middle half of the seven-year Tribulation. The Tribulation is a set time of seven years and is divided into two equal halves of 42 months each—1,260 days followed by another 1,260 days. During this midpoint of the seven years, a man called the Antichrist will lead a military invasion of northeastern Africa.

He will seize control of Egypt, Libya and Ethiopia (Daniel 11:42, 43). He will march an Islamic army into Israel and, using the Palestinian people and their resources, again divide the holy city into East and West Jerusalem. He will take total possession of the Temple Mount in Jerusalem, where he will be hailed as a hero among his Muslim brothers (Revelation 11:1, 2).

This Antichrist is identified in Daniel as a little horn with "a mouth speaking great things" (Daniel 7:8). He will become "strong with a small people" (Daniel 11:23), and will control 10 future kings and their kingdoms (Revelation 13:1). The success of the coming Antichrist will come through his ability to go to war and continually come out a victor. Twice, Revelation 13 mentions his ability to make war (Revelation 13:4, 7).

Much has been written about the Antichrist since John penned the Book of Revelation, and the early church fathers gave us four centuries of commentaries on it, In comparison, however, little has been taught about a man Revelation identifies as the "False Prophet." In fact, many of the reformers, including Martin Luther, taught that the Antichrist would be a pope.

There are two beasts, or unusual men, that John sees in his vision in Revelation 13, however. The first (verse 1) is the beast rising out of the sea, and the second (verse 11) is a beast rising out of the earth.

These "beasts" represent two separate people, as indicated by the use of the pronouns *he, him* and *his* (Revelation 13:3, 4; 13:11-18).

The wording of the text makes it impossible to make this prediction symbolic or allegorical. They are always identified with masculine pronouns—never with a neuter term such as *it.* Below is the first mention of the second beast that is later identified as the "false prophet."

> *Then I saw another beast coming up out of the earth, and he had two horns like a lamb and spoke like a dragon. And he exercises all the authority of the first beast in his presence, and causes the earth and those who dwell in it to worship the first beast, whose deadly wound was healed. He performs great signs, so that he even makes fire come down from heaven on the earth in the sight of men.*
>
> *And he deceives those who dwell on the earth by those signs which he was granted to do in the sight of the beast, telling those who dwell on the earth to make an image to the beast who was wounded by the sword and lived.*
>
> *He was granted power to give breath to the image of the beast, that the image of the beast should both speak and cause as many as would not worship the image of the beast to be killed. He causes all, both small and great, rich and poor, free and slave, to receive a mark on their right hand or on their foreheads* (Revelation 13:11-16).

Seizing Control of Jerusalem

The Biblical prophecies indicate that Jerusalem will be a "cup of trembling" or drunkenness to all nations in the future (Zechariah 12:2). Jerusalem is sacred to three monotheistic religions: Judaism, Christianity and Islam. The Temple Mount is also sacred to all three groups.

Among the Jews, the mountain of God is holy since both Jewish Temple compounds were erected there. The Christians revere the mountain as the site of Christ's crucifixion and Resurrection. To the Muslims, tradition says this mountain is the place where Muhammad ascended to heaven from his horse during what Islam calls "The Night Vision."

Today, Christians and Jews are forbidden to pray, worship, read the Bible or the Torah on the Temple Mount. Two Islamic Mosques cover the southern and central areas of the mountain. To the south sits the Al Aqsa, and the golden Dome of the Rock towers over the center of the sacred platform. Although Jerusalem has changed hands several times during military conflicts, the Muslims today maintain clear and undisputed control of the entire Temple Mount area.

The main keg of dynamite set to ignite the Middle East into a burning inferno is the question of who controls the sacred mountain in Jerusalem. In the Six-Day War of 1967, Israeli troops seized Arab East Jerusalem and the Temple Mount. For the first time since Israel had again become a nation, Jewish military vehicles rumbled across the ancient hills near the Dome of the Rock and Israeli paratroopers planted a temporary Israeli flag on the Mount near the Western Wall.

Chief Rabbi Sholomo Goren marched to the Western Wall, located just below the Temple compound, and blew the shofar in the midst of Israeli soldiers who were shouting, crying and praying at the Wall, one of the holiest prayer sites in all of Judaism.

One of the heroes of the Six-Day War, a one-eyed general named Moshe Dayan had in his control the keys that unlocked the gates of the Temple Mount. At that time it was under the control of the Jordanians. Shortly after the war concluded, Dayan gave the keys to the Temple Mount gate back to the Islamic Wakf.

There are Israeli military personnel who, to this day, have not forgiven Dayan for not seizing control of the mountain where the two Jewish Temples once stood.

The General however, was aware that any Israeli seizure of Islam's third holiest mosque would immediately bring the wrath of a billion Muslims against the young Jewish state. In the interest of keeping the future peace, the country of Jordan maintained control of the Temple Mount. Today, it still sits behind the old walls of Jerusalem.

Both Jerusalem and the ancient hill called Mount Moriah, the acreage housing both Islamic Mosques, will become the center of focus at the time of the end. Both the coming Antichrist and the False Prophet of the Apocalypse will be directly involved in matters pertaining to Jerusalem and the holy mountain.

Since the battle for Jerusalem will be a conflict of religions, it clearly identifies the future ringleader of the coming conflict.

Important Clues from Revelation 13

The first interesting point in these passages is that throughout the New Testament and the Book of Revelation the symbol of a lamb is used to identify Christ. The word *lamb* is used 29 times in the Book of Revelation alone. Twenty-eight of those times, the word *lamb* links Jesus Christ with the priestly ministry He gained through His earthly sufferings.

Christ was called the "Lamb of God" by John the Baptist, and He died near the time of Passover, the very feast of Judaism that centers on the Passover lamb and Israel's deliverance from Egypt (John 1:29; Exodus 12; Matthew 26:2). Only in Revelation 13:11 does the symbol of the lamb NOT represent Jesus, but identifies the character of a future man who will represent a perverted or apostate form of the Christian faith.

John identifies this man with the symbolism of a lamb with two horns. In prophetic symbolism, horns can represent an empire, a kingdom, a leader or political and spiritual authority. These meanings are seen in the prophecies of Daniel and Revelation.

The future Antichrist is symbolized as a beast with 10 horns. These 10 horns represent 10 future kings ruling over 10 nations (Daniel 7:24; Revelation 17:12). Since the "lamb with two horns" is a religious leader (a *false prophet*, Revelation 20:10), the two horns indicate he will oversee *two religions* from Jerusalem. To which religions do the two horns allude?

We easily discover which two religions are the largest and strongest in this area of the former Roman Empire. In Western Europe and the Middle East the two prominent religions are Catholicism and Islam. Islam is the main political/religious force dominating Northern Africa, and much of the Middle East.

The traditional Roman Catholic Church is still strong throughout much of Western and Eastern Europe, although in recent years there has been a sharp decline in church attendance. After much research and personal observation I believe the False Prophet will be an apostate religious leader, perhaps emerging out of the Roman Church. This theory has been propagated by several leading Roman Catholics for many years. Here are some quotes indicating the identity of the false prophet of the Apocalypse.

Pope Pius X wrote 82 years ago:

> *There is a good reason to fear that the coming great apostasy may be the foretaste of a defecting Pontiff-Pope. It will be the beginning of those evils reserved for the last days. This Son of Perdition, mentioned in 2 Thessalonians 2:3, may already be in the world.*

Saint Vincent said:

> *Just before the end of the world, an agent of Christ will become an agent of the Antichrist to gain influence and wealth.*

Saint Francis of Assisi wrote:

> *There will be an invalidly elected Pope. He will cause great confusion. He will cause Catholics to doubt their faith. He will accept all religions on equal basis. There will be widespread dissent, and he will deceive even the very elect if the last days are not shortened.*

Archbishop Fulton J. Sheen said:

> *The False Prophet will have a religion without a cross, a religion without a world to come, a religion to destroy religions. There will be a counter church, Christ's church will be one and the False Prophet will create the other. The False Church will be ecumenical global and worldly. . . . The mystical body on earth today will have its Judas Iscariot and he will be the False Prophet. . . . He will sell the mystical body to the Antichrist.*

Cardinal John J. O'Conner declared in "The Reign of the False Prophet" that the universal teaching of church fathers, under the classification of sacred tradition, is that "this final False Prophet will be a bishop of the church and will lead all religions into becoming one."

Muslims and Christians Merging

It may seem impossible for Muslims and any form of Christianity to merge. Catholic publications, such as *Soul Magazine*, the voice of the Cultus of Mary, continually emphasize in articles the association Mary has with Muslims. The Knights of Eternal Wisdom explain their mission with a logo:

This logo represents Christians, Muslims and Jews who become warriors for God uniting faith, hope and love as they put on the armor of God. . . . The helmet of the Knights is shaped as an "M" to symbolize that Christians, Muslims and Jews are united with Mary.

Supernatural, Counterfeit Miracles

This False Prophet will demonstrate to the world his supernatural power through two demon-inspired miracles. He will make "fire come down from heaven on the earth in the sight of men" (Revelation 13:13). He will create an image of the Beast, then cause the image to speak and live in the sight of men (Revelation 13:15).

These two false miracles will demonstrate the "power, signs, and lying wonders" the apostle Paul warned of in 2 Thessalonians 2:9. The creation of this image of the Beast is the strong delusion that will deceive the world and cause many to believe a lie and be condemned because they do not love the truth (2 Thessalonians 2:11, 12).

The Icon of the Beast

John wrote Revelation 13, alluding to the "image" of the Beast. He wrote in Koine Greek because it was, in that day, the common language of the people. John could have selected either of three Greek words to identify the meaning of the word *image*. He could have used the Greek word *charakter*, which means "to cut or to stamp out an image," or the word *charagma,* which alludes to engraved art. Instead, he used the Greek word *eikon* to identify the image.

Note that this "image of the Beast" is not a painting or a picture of the Antichrist. The Greek word *eikon* means "a statue in the likeness of something or someone." From this same Greek word, we derive the English word *icon.*

In Greek and Russian Orthodox churches, an icon is a picture or painting of an early saint, the disciples, or Christ. In Catholic churches an icon can be an actual statue of Jesus, the disciples, Mary, or a saint.

This particular icon will not be an image of Jesus, Mary or His disciples; it will be an icon made in the image of the future Antichrist. The Bible indicates that in the final days of the seven-year Tribulation, many will be deceived by this false Christ and many will accept these demonic miracles as miracles from God (see 2 Thessalonians 2).

Commands Against Images in Worship

Two main branches of Islam are the Sunnis and the Shiites. The Sunni branch of the Islamic religion does not use any form of pictures in their worship. The Shiite branch of Muslims, however, in areas such as Iran can often be seen holding pictures of their imams and holy men during protests and religious festivals.

In the Old Testament, pagan religions would often carve images out of trees in high places and burn incense to false idols (Leviticus 26:30; 2 Kings 16:2-4; Isaiah 65:3-7). God is Spirit, however, and must be worshiped in spirit and in truth (John 4:24).

In countries where Hindus worship images, such as India, it is commonly reported that the statues of these idols manifest tears, blood or some other counterfeit miracle to draw the followers of the religion deeper into the worship of the idol.

I must point out that God's Word strictly forbids the building of any form of an image. Notice the following warning given to the ancient Hebrews:

> *Take careful heed to yourselves, for you saw no form when the Lord spoke to you at Horeb out of the midst of the fire, lest you act corruptly and make for yourselves a carved image in the form of any figure: the likeness of male or female, the likeness of any animal that is on the earth or the likeness of any winged bird that flies in the air, the likeness of anything that creeps on the ground or the likeness of any fish that is in the water beneath the earth. And take heed, lest you lift your eyes to heaven, and when you see the sun, the moon, and the stars, all the host of heaven, you feel driven to worship them and serve them, which the Lord your God has given to all the peoples under the whole heaven as a heritage. But the Lord has taken you and brought you out of the iron furnace, out of Egypt, to be His people, an inheritance, as you are this day* (Deuteronomy 4:15-20).

When the Jews were commanded to build the Tabernacle in the wilderness, and centuries later Solomon constructed the elaborate Temple in Jerusalem, there was no picture or image of a person, or a beast permitted to be built into or painted on walls in any area of the Temple.

This was to ensure that people wouldn't worship an image. One of the greatest deceptions Satan can create can be through images and statues.

Men have often been exposed to elaborate hoaxes involving religious images and statues, including images linked to the Roman Church.

- *In Lomello, Italy, for example, a plaster image of the Virgin Mary began to weep, drawing thousands of the faithful to the home of the owner. It was later discovered that the owner had a squirt gun he was using to produce the red tears.*
- *In Canada, there was the manifestation of a statue of the Virgin dripping blood from December, 1985 through January, 1986. After thorough research, it was discovered that the blood was a mixture of vegetable oil and beef fat that had been tinted with red coloring.*
- *In January 1974, an image of John F. Kennedy began weeping in Pescara, Italy. Someone was wise enough to have the alleged blood tested, and it was discovered that, sure enough, it was human blood; but it was in an advanced decomposed state. In other words, someone had taken human blood and placed it on the image.*

In a famous church in the Holy Land there was an old painting of Christ's face on one of the columns in the church. Word spread that the painting was weeping. Immediately, hundreds of locals, followed by thousands of pilgrims, gathered to see this "miracle" and bring their offerings to the church.

I asked a Palestinian friend of mine who was familiar with the church, the members and the priest, about this alleged miracle. He laughed and said:

> *The church needed a new roof, so the priest shot water on the painting with a squirt gun. Needless to say, when he began yelling, "The face is weeping," pilgrims and offerings poured so people could see "signs and wonders" in the old church.*

In the first century the Christian church had no images of Christ or saints. From A.D. 100 to 400, early Christian leaders rebuked those who sought to introduce images into Christian worship. The 36th synod of Elvira in the fourth century prohibited images in worship, calling them a hindrance to the worship to God. Eusebius, an early church father, opposed images.

In the time of Augustine, Jerome and Ambrose, images were introduced in the church, especially in the eastern branch of the church. From about 766 onward, many leaders in the church not only accepted images but used them in veneration in worship.

This action is an outright violation of the warnings given by the Almighty in the Scriptures (Exodus 23:24; 34:13; Numbers 33:51-53).

One of the Ten Commandments was, "you shall not make yourself any graven image" (Exodus 20:4, *Amp.*). Some suggest that these warnings are just for Israel, or that they are listed in the Old Testament and therefore are not valid in contemporary times. The New Testament, however, gives the same warnings against idol worship:

> *[Turn] to God from idols to serve the living and true God* (1 Thessalonians 1:9).
>
> *Keep yourself from idols* (1 John 5:21).
>
> *They should not worship demons, and idols of gold, silver, brass, stone, and wood, which can neither see nor hear nor walk* (Revelation 9:20).

The inspired Scriptures also forbid praying to idols (Leviticus 19:4; 1 Kings 18:22-29), performing rites to the dead (Deuteronomy 14:1), burning incense to idols (Exodus 30:9), and kissing or bowing down to an image (1 Kings 19:18). Any religious image, whether it represents Hinduism, Buddhism, Islam or Christianity, that appears to bleed, cry or move is a counterfeit miracle because the Holy Spirit will never go against the revelation and warnings of the Holy Scriptures.

False miracles cause a person to be drawn deeper in to that particular religion and lead to further acceptance of other images that manifest some form of "living."

Is it possible that the emphasis on images in the Roman Church has unknowingly and unwittingly prepared masses of people in Europe and the Middle East to accept a future miracle of the talking and living image of the Beast?

John tells us that this image of the Beast will speak and live, causing multitudes to worship the image (icon). When Moses built the brazen serpent in the wilderness, Israel looked on the serpent, a picture of Christ on the Cross, and they were healed (Numbers 21).

Israel preserved this brass serpent in the Temple for 900 years and began to burn incense to it. In the time of King Hezekiah, the godly leader destroyed the holy relic because it had become an idol to the Jews (2 Kings 18:4). God hates idolatry!

We often hear about the "Mark of the Beast," and how that no man can buy or sell without the *name,* the *number* or the *mark* of the Beast (Revelation 13:16-18). For years I have heard ministers say that this mark will be initiated by the Antichrist himself. However, if you pay careful attention to the wording of the Biblical prophecy, it reveals that the "he" who causes all to receive a mark is the False Prophet, not the Antichrist.

An Image That Speaks and Lives (Images and Miracles)

This mark will be connected to the Beast and his system, but it will be initiated by the False Prophet. It will be used to unite the religious followers of the Antichrist and the followers of the False Prophet into one social, religious and economic unit. A person can buy, sell and have food to eat if they participate in the worship of the image of the Beast and receive its mark, number or name.

There have been numerous manmade "miracles" performed in the name of religion. The future image of this Beast, however, will not be a miracle performed by human trickery or slick illusions. The Bible says of this event, "The coming of the lawless one is according to the working of Satan, with all power, signs, and lying wonders" (2 Thessalonians 2:9).

Jesus warned that false Christs would deceive many (Matthew 24:24). All religions have what they consider "miracles." Even in the Islamic religion, there are certain groups noted for strange and bizarre "miracles." One Islamic group, called the **Dervish,** lives in the region of Persia (Iran) and Turkey.

There are several sub-sects of dervishes, but the original Islamic sect was formed in 1165 and organized in 1273. They are a very secretive group who chant and work themselves into an emotional frenzy during their prayer time. One group is called the *Howling Dervishes.*

Once they are in the religious frenzy they can eat glass without cutting their mouths or tongues, lie on a bed of nails without piercing their skin, walk on hot coals without burning their feet, handle red-hot iron and eat red-hot coals without apparent harm and perform other strange feats. Those who have observed members of this group say they are unrivaled in the art of magic, hypnotism and sorcery.

The Antichrist will use the occult to his advantage. According to Daniel 8:25: "Through his policy also he shall cause craft (deceit) to prosper in his hand" (KJV).

The Bible calls the false prophet a "beast coming up out of the earth" (Revelation 13:11). The Greek word for beast is *therion*, and means a "wild beast or a dangerous animal." In Biblical terms, the use of *beast* is symbolism, indicating the wild nature of the person. Ironically, Muslims have a belief that a "beast" will call people back to Islam at the time that Isa, or Jesus, appears.

The University of Southern California sponsored a lecture by Islamic scholar Gharm-Allah el-Ghandy who detailed the "Signs of the Last Hour" from the perspective of Islam. Here are some excerpts from the notes distributed:

> *Isa (Jesus) will come at the time of al-Dajja; and al-Mahdi as well. He will descend at the time of Fajr prayer on a masjid in Damascus, the capital of Syria. He is of medium height, red-faced, and his hair is as if he just took a shower. He will call people back to Islam, but he will also be a military leader.*
>
> *The people of the Book (Bible) will revert to Islam, and wealth will be super-abundant. Isa (Jesus) will break the cross, kill the swine, and personally slay Al-Dajjal (Antichrist). He will stay on earth for a long time thereafter.*
>
> *An animal will come and call people back to Islam. (A partial description of this animal is that it is very hairy, so much so that one will not be able to tell its front from its rear [Arabic: Dab-ba]. Reference to this animal is mentioned in the Qur'an.)*

Could this image that will speak and live actually instruct people to unite as one unit? Will this be the expected beast that Islam is anticipating? If the Antichrist is a Muslim and the False Prophet an apostate Catholic, how then will the Jewish people fit into this scenario? This question is especially pertinent since the counterfeit miracles will be occurring in Jerusalem, the spiritual capital of Israel. The speaking image may be linked to a Jewish legend of the *golem*.

The Creation of the *Golem*

In Hebrew, *golem* means a "shapeless mass." The Talmud uses the word as "unformed" or "imperfect." According to Talmudic legend, Adam is called *golem,* meaning "a body without a soul" (Sanhedrin 38b). The word appears only once in the Bible.

The formal meaning of the word is "an animated being created from an inanimate mass." In Psalm 139:16, David said God saw him in his mother's womb when he was still a *golem*, or a shapeless mass of tissue.

For several years the image has been linked in Jewish folklore to the Creation, and to a famous Jewish legend about a *golem*.

The earth was first created in a shapeless mass ("without form, and void"). Over the centuries the legend grew and became associated with the figure of a giant being. According to the Jewish legend, a Jewish scholar and teacher in the 16th century brought to life a giant man, formed from clay, called a *golem*. The *golem's* task was to destroy those who were persecuting the Jews living in the city of Prague, Czechoslovakia.

At the time, Jews were being persecuted throughout Europe. Jewish enemies accused them of mixing the blood of Christian children in their flour and water, when making the Jewish *matzo* bread. This lie, known as the "Blood Lie," incited mobs to retaliate against Jews living in the region. The chief rabbi of Prague, Judah Loew ben Bezalel, realized that violence and danger were coming.

One night he dreamed the city was covered in fire and lying in ruins. In the smoke and ashes, the word *golem* was written. The rabbi knew that a *golem* was a giant made out of clay because the mystics of the Jewish religion spoke frequently of the legend. The creature, so says the tradition, could be created but only by a *tsadik*, or a righteous man.

According to the legend, the rabbi took his son-in-law, Itzak Kohen and his top student, Yakov Sasson, to the clay banks of the Moldau River at darkness. By midnight, they had sculped a giant body out of the river clay. It lay before them, lifeless.

The rabbi then prayed, using mystical words and the sacred name of God (*YHVH*). Storm clouds immediately gathered and lightning danced in the sky. The creature began to move. The rabbi then knelt and wrote on the forehead of the creature the Hebrew word *emet*, which means truth. He commanded, "*Golem*, awake!"

The legend continues that the rabbi kept the *golem* in his house. He instructed it to protect the Jews and expose and capture those telling lies on the Jews. He named the *golem* Joseph.

The *golem*, according to the legend, exposed the Jew-haters. Eventually, the people of Prague became involved in a civil conflict that began to grow rapidly. The rabbi met with the head of the City of Prague at his castle, and agreed to destroy the *golem* if the Jews were guaranteed their safety.

The rabbi proceeded to destroy the *golem* by erasing the Hebrew letter *alef*, the first letter in the word *emet* on its forehead. Then the word spelled *met*, a Hebrew word for *death*. Thus, the *golem* came to its end. It was said that the clay was then placed in the attic of the rabbi's synagogue. To this day, a tourist who visits Prague can see small images and cards with paintings of *golems*.

This legend had prompted some students of prophecy to speculate that the future False Prophet could be from a Jewish background who is familiar with the legend of the *golem*. Since the *golem* allegedly came to life after the three Hebrew letters, *alef, mem* and *tav* were written on the *forehead,* this could be linked to the mark of the beast, a mark that is made in the right hand or in the forehead (Revelation 13:17-18)!

The Temple Mount and the False Prophet

In the heart of the old city of Jerusalem, behind the old eastern wall, is the Temple Mount, a 27-acre piece of flat property that once held the sacred Jewish Temples of Solomon and Herod. At some point in the future, the Temple Mount in Jerusalem will become ground zero for the greatest spiritual deception and conflict in history. This site is sacred to the Jews, the Christians and the Muslims. At this present time there is no Jewish Temple on the Temple Mount in Jerusalem.

Two Islamic mosques are there, however—the golden "Dome of the Rock" and the "Al Aqsa Mosque." But Biblical prophecies indicate that a Temple will be built there during the tribulation (Revelation 11:1, 2). Presently, several Jewish groups are gaining influence and popularity inside and outside of Israel, and are interested in a future Jewish Temple in Jerusalem.

One group, the Treasures of the Temple Institute, has re-created many of the gold and silver vessels used in the Temple worship, including, more recently, the garment of the High Priest. Other smaller, yet outspoken, groups, such as the Temple Mount Faithful, continually speak of Jewish rights to the Temple Mount and have made unsuccessful attempts to move a large limestone cornerstone to the Mount as a foundation stone for a new Temple.

This future Temple will be constructed during the Tribulation. This is the same Temple area John was told to measure in Revelation 11:1, 2. I personally believe that the actual rebuilding of a future Jewish Temple is linked to the appearance and the ministry of the famous two witnesses of Revelation 11.

This passage in Revelation which speaks of the measurement of the (earthly) Temple reveals how the Gentiles would trample Jerusalem for 42 months. Most scholars agree with Scriptures that identify Elijah as one of the two witnesses to appear in Jerusalem during the first half of the Tribulation (see Malachi 4:5).

Jesus mentioned that Elijah would come and "restore all things" (Matthew 17:11). It appears that one aspect of Elijah's ministry may be to help initiate the rebuilding of a future Jewish Temple on the Temple Mount.

This rebuilding will transpire during the first 42 months of the Tribulation, and the actual Temple "dedication" will be interrupted by an invasion of the Antichrist who kills the two witnesses (Revelation 11:7), thus becoming a hero among the Muslims as he takes complete control of the sacred mountain. The enemies of Israel rejoice (Revelation 11:10).

Once the Antichrist seizes total control of east Jerusalem and the Temple Mount, the False Prophet will join him and multitudes will worship the man as though he were God (2 Thessalonians 2:3, 4). At this point, the false prophet will construct the icon (image) of the Beast. On completion, he causes the image to speak and live.

Religious Jews in Jerusalem at this time will see this "miracle," a demonic manifestation that causes an "abomination" that makes Jerusalem desolate (Matthew 24:15). Daniel predicted this abomination in his prophecies:

He will confirm a covenant with many for one "seven." In the middle of the "seven" he will put an end to sacrifice and offering. And on a wing of the temple he will set up an abomination that causes desolation, until the end that is decreed is poured out on him (Daniel 9:27, *NIV*).

This prediction by Daniel was recognized centuries later during the writing of the New Testament. Jesus spoke about the signs of his coming. Matthew pointed out the prophecy of Daniel when he wrote:

When you see the "abomination of desolation," spoken of by Daniel the prophet, standing in the holy place (whoever reads, let him understand) (Matthew 24:15).

Matthew admitted he was uncertain of the meaning of Daniel's prophecy. This is because Matthew's gospel was written in about A.D. 50, and the revelation of the full meaning of the image of the Beast was not given to John until A.D. 95, over 45 years after Matthew recorded his Gospel. Neither Daniel and Matthew had full understanding concerning this "abomination."

The Law of Moses reveals, however, that idolatry and idol worship are classified as abominations (Deuteronomy 7:25, 26; 12:29-31; 13:12-17). Many commentaries agree that the primary meaning of abomination is idolatry or idol worship.

The Hebrew text of Daniel's prophecy teaches that in the middle of the seven-year Tribulation an abomination will be set up on the "wing of the Temple" (Daniel 9:27). This could allude to the corner of the *new* Temple structure yet to be built, or it may allude to the southeastern corner of the present wall of the Temple Mount. The latter is known as the "pinnacle of the Temple."

From either vantage point, hundreds of thousands of "worshipers" could visibly see the image and watch as the False Prophet performed his feats of false miracles. I can imagine the image of the Beast positioned on the wing of the Temple for worshipers to see.

Suddenly, this manmade icon begins to move and speak in the sight of men. Multitudes will be deceived into believing that Christ himself has now returned to Jerusalem and is manifesting His presence for the world.

This would also fulfill the ancient expectations of the Islamic religion that teaches that Jesus (Isa) will appear in Jerusalem and deny He was God's son.

The "lamb with two horns" will effectively pull all apostate Christians and Muslims into his grasp. He will do this by denying the *deity* of Christ, by persecuting the Jews and by killing anyone who refuses to worship the image of the Beast.

This scenario will play well into the hands of any Muslim throughout the world.

> *He was granted power to give breath to the image of the beast, that the image of the beast should both speak and cause as many as would not worship the image of the beast to be killed* (Revelation 13:15).

Death for non-worshipers will come by beheading (Revelation 20:4). This is the 1,400-year-old method used in strict Islamic nations for capital crimes against the government or Islam. The Islamic link to many troublesome prophecies is undeniable.

Who is this false prophet? What is his religious background? According to many Catholic and Protestant leaders, this "lamb with two horns" will rise out of the Roman Catholic Church system, at a time when the church enters a severe period of spiritual disintegration and corruption.

For many walk, of whom I have told you often, and now tell you even weeping, that they are the enemies of the cross of Christ (Philippians 3:18).

6

Merging the Crescent with the Broken Cross

Sitting atop mosques throughout the world is the universal emblem of the Islamic religion, the crescent moon. Perched high on church steeples around the globe is a cross, the universal emblem of Christ's death and His defeat of Satan through the crucifixion.

Islamists deny that Christ was ever crucified or died on the Cross. They teach that another person who looked like Jesus was crucified in His place. Therefore, the Cross is an offense to a Muslim, and the crescent is viewed as the dominant symbol of their control globally. At present, it seems foolish to project the idea that in the future certain groups of Muslims and an apostate form of Christianity could merge in the Middle East, especially in Jerusalem.

Most western Christians, however, are unaware of the link between Muslims, Catholics and Orthodox Christians in Egypt, Jordan, Syria, Lebanon and Israel. When you remove the fanatical Islamic element from the picture, many of the common, more secular Muslims are actually friendly to, and receptive of, Roman and Orthodox believers and priests.

For example, many of the Muslims in the Holy Land actually attended Catholic schools as children in areas such as Bethlehem and the West Bank. A Palestinian friend informed me that a Catholic priest would visit Muslims who were sick and pray for them in the hospital. Muslims would kiss the rosary (prayer beads) if the priest removed the cross.

They were not offended to kiss the image of Mary on the rosary, but they would never kiss the cross, which, as stated, is an offense to them.

The great mystery is how a future apostate Pope and a future Islamic leader will join together, when there is a great divide over the deity, death and resurrection of Christ? A Catholic is taught to believe that Jesus was born of the Virgin Mary and that he was the Son of God (Matthew 1:23; Matthew 16:16). They must believe Jesus died and was raised from the dead for the forgiveness of sins to be a Christian.

Muslims, however, accept Jesus as a prophet but deny completely that Christ is the Son of God. They teach that God has no son. The Roman church must change a major doctrine before these two groups can merge. That doctrine would be the belief of who Jesus is.

For a Muslim to completely accept a so-called "Christian" leader, that leader would need to deny that Jesus was God's son and deny that Jesus was ever crucified and raised from the dead. Some may say this will never happen; however, some church leaders in England, Europe and the Middle East are already saying, publicly, that Jesus was not the Son of God!

Both Muslims and Christians believe that Jesus was born of the Virgin Mary. In the Koran, Jesus is called "Isa bin Maryim," or "Jesus the son of Mary." The Qur'an, however, makes these negative statements about Jesus being the son of God:

> *O People of the Book! Commit no excesses in your religion: nor say of Allah aught but the truth. Christ Jesus the son of Mary was (no more than) an apostle of Allah* (Surah 4:171).

In blasphemy indeed are those that say that God is the Messiah the son of Mary (Surah 5:17).

> *They say, "God has taken to Himself a son." You have no authority for this. What do you say concerning God that you know not? Say: "Those who forge a lie against God shall not be successful." We shall make them taste severe punishment because they disbelieved* (Surah 10:68-70).

> *And warn those who say, "God has taken a son." A grievous word it is that comes out of their mouths; they speak nothing but a lie* (Surah 18:4, 5).

Secrets Inside the Dome of the Rock

On the Temple Mount in Jerusalem sits the third holiest Islamic mosque in the world, the Dome of the Rock. Inside this mosque are quotes in Arabic accredited to Muhammad and the Qur'an. Recently they were translated into English so that English-speaking Muslims would understand their meaning. On the inner face of the South wall are these words:

In the name of Allah, the Merciful, the Compassionate. There is no God but Allah alone; he has no associate. Unto Him belongs sovereignty and unto Him belongs praise. He is the Kingship and to Him belongeth praise. He quickens to life and He gives death; and He has Power over all things.

Moving counterclockwise, these words are on the Southeast wall:

Lo! Allah and His angels shower blessings on the Prophet. O ye who believe! Ask blessings on him and salute him with a worthy salutation. O People of the Book! Do not exaggerate in your religion nor utter aught concerning the truth.

The East wall has this inscription:

The Messiah, Jesus son of Mary, was only a Messenger of God, and His Word which He conveyed unto Mary, and a spirit from Him. So believe in God and His messengers, and say not "Three" (Trinity). Cease! It is better for you!

The Northeast wall contains these words:

God is only One God. Far be it removed from His transcendent majesty that He should have a son.

His is all that is in the heavens and all that is in the earth. And God is sufficient as Defender. The Messiah will never scorn to be a servant unto God, nor will the favored angels.

On the North wall:

He who scorns His service and is proud, all such will He assemble unto Him. Oh Allah, bless Your Messenger and Your servant Jesus, the son of Mary.

The Northwest wall has these words:

Peace be on him the day he was born, and the day he dies, and the day he shall be raised alive! Such was Jesus, son of Mary, (this is) a statement of the truth concerning which they doubt. It does not befit the Majesty of Allah that He should take unto Himself a son. Glory be to Him!

Muslims have inscribed on the inside West wall of the Dome of the Rock:

When Allah decrees a thing, He says to it only: Be! and it is. Lo! Allah is my Lord and your Lord. So serve Him. That is the right path. Allah himself is witness that there is no god save Him. And the angels and the men of learning are also witness. Maintaining His creation in justice, there is no God save Him, the Almighty, the Wise.

On the outside western wall of the mosque are these words:

In the name of Allah, the Merciful and Compassionate. There is no god but Allah alone. Praise be Allah who has not taken unto himself a son and who has no partner in sovereignty, nor has he any protector on

> *account of weakness. Muhammad is the messenger of Allah, may God pray upon Him and accept his intercession.*

Finally, on the inside of the southwest wall are these words:

> *Lo! religion with God is Islam. Those who received the Book differed only after knowledge came to them, through transgression among themselves. He who does not believe the revelations of God will find that lo! God is swift at reckoning!*

Islam is adamant on the issue of who Jesus is. To them, he is not in any manner or form the Son of God. He is one of the great prophets and that is all. The false prophet of Revelation may do more than deny the deity of Christ; he may go so far as to announce that he is the Christ who has returned to earth!

Jesus' Divinity in Question

Should the divinity of Jesus be denied by a future Roman church leader, he would be received warmly by the world's Muslims. If he further teaches that Christ was never crucified and raised from the dead, he would be highly revered as a man who has received the true revelation from Allah, which agrees with the Islamic teaching and concept of Jesus!

The Cross of Christ is the dividing issue between Muslims and Christians. Both groups believe in prayer, fasting, giving to the poor, heaven and hell, and the last days. But Muslims teach that Muhammad was the final prophet of God and that their holy book, the Qur'an (not the Bible), is God's final revelation to mankind.

They also believe that Jesus was never crucified. When the time came for the crucifixion, they allege, Jesus was taken to heaven and a person who appeared to look like Christ was actually crucified in His place. When Jesus appeared before God, he was rebuked by God who asked Jesus, "Why did you tell people you were My son, when you know I have no sons?"

According to Islamic belief, Jesus repented and God told him He would appear on earth at the end of days and tell the world He lied and He was *not* the Son of God. To prove the point, Muslims contend that Jesus will then deny the teaching of the Trinity, tear down the crosses and kill the swine (the Jews).

It is possible that the future False Prophet may fulfill the expectations of over 1.4 billion Muslims. He may actually present himself as Jesus Christ! There have been a few disillusioned religious kooks throughout history who claimed to be Jesus. They presented no "proof" to confirm their impersonation, however.

The False Prophet will perform two astonishing miracles that sweep millions of New Agers, Hindus and Muslims into his fold. They will be creating the image of the Beast and calling down fire from heaven in the sight of men (Revelation 13:13-15). The miracle of calling fire down from heaven in the sight of men will demonstrate his supernatural ability to control nature. The miracle of the icon shows his control over life itself.

To the world, this talking image will surpass any miracle recorded in the four gospels that was performed by the historic Christ. During Christ's 42 months of ministry, he raised several people from the dead. However, Christ never performed a miracle causing an image or a statue to speak and live. This would be idolatry which is forbidden by God. Christ would never operate outside the will of his Heavenly Father, the Almighty.

The False Prophet will demonstrate to the world an ability that seems to be equal to God himself. He will create an icon of the Beast (Antichrist) and by demonic manifestation, will cause the image to speak and live.

People who live in a contemporary, modern society may be more apt to question the credibility of such a "miracle." Those living in India, much of eastern Europe and the Middle East, however, could easily be swayed into worshiping this talking image and accepting it as a sign from God that "Jesus has returned to earth."

Ask a Muslim if he believes in Jesus and he will say, "Of course." He may even tell you he believes that Jesus will return to earth again and appear in Jerusalem. The Jesus of Islam, however, is not the Jesus of the New Testament, although Muslims would say He is. When the true Christ of the Cross reappears on the Mount of Olives in Jerusalem, He will bear in His body the scars of His suffering.

The Biblical prophet writes about this:

> *And I will pour on the house of David and on the inhabitants of Jerusalem the Spirit of grace and*

> *supplication; then they will look on Me whom they pierced. Yes, they will mourn for Him as one mourns for his only son, and grieve for Him as one grieves for a firstborn* (Zechariah 12:10).
>
> *And one will say to him, "What are these wounds between your arms?" Then he will answer, "Those with which I was wounded in the house of my friends"* (Zechariah 13:6).

The major difference you can visually see between the Jesus of the Bible and the Jesus of Islam will be the wounds in the hands of the Messiah! Islam denies the crucifixion; therefore, wounds aren't necessary to prove to the Islamic world that this man performing miracles is actually Jesus. Jesus warned, "False prophets will rise up and deceive many" (Matthew 24:11). Later, He said:

> *False christs and false prophets will rise and show great signs and wonders to deceive, if possible, even the elect* (Matthew 24:24).

How Will They Worship the Beast?

The apostle Paul also warned that a man of sin would arise. His coming would be after the working of Satan, and he would be accompanied by lying signs and wonders that would deceive (2 Thessalonians 2:9). New Testament warnings make it clear that the counterfeit miracles of the future False Prophet will seize the minds of the entire world and cause multitudes to follow both beasts, the Antichrist *and* the False Prophet.

The coming False Prophet will demand that the world worship the Beast and his icon (Revelation 13:12). The apostle John used the word "worship" twice in Revelation 13, both times in reference to the worship of the beast and his image (icon). The Greek language has as many as eight different words that were used when speaking of worship or worshiping God, a person or a thing.

The word used in Revelation 13 is *proskuneo.* It comes from two Greek words, *pros,* meaning "toward," and *kuneo,* meaning "to kiss." Worship means, literally, to kiss toward, or pay great homage or respect toward something. In the New Testament Roman period, the word would have been used when a person would kiss the ring of the Roman emperor. Throughout the Bible, when a person would worship they would often bow before God.

Idolaters bow to an idol in worship. In Daniel 3:3, people bowed to the image and in Daniel 3:5, the people fell down and worshiped this image built by Nebuchadnezzar. In John's day, Roman emperors accepted worship as a god. Worshiping the emperor was common, and it was meant to flatter the ruler.

The worship of the Antichrist is a central theme in the Revelation, and John makes six references to it:

> *And they worshiped the beast* (Revelation 13:4).

> *All who dwell on the earth will worship [the Beast], whose names have not been written in the Book of Life* (Revelation 13:8).

And causes the earth and those who dwell in it to worship the first beast (Revelation 13:12).

If anyone worships the beast and his image (Revelation 14:9).

They have no rest day or night, who worship the beast and his image (Revelation 14:11).

Who had not worshiped the beast or his image (Revelation 20:4).

The Vatican's Link to Jerusalem

You may believe it is impossible for the Roman Church and Islam to link together. Consider, however, that the Roman Church owns huge amounts of property, including historic churches, throughout Jerusalem, especially in the eastern section not far from the Temple Mount. Information released in June, 1996, through the International Christian Embassy, spoke of rumors circulating in Israel of a link between certain members of Israel's government and the Vatican.

The rumor stated that there was interest in allowing Jerusalem to be the political capital of Israel, while allowing parts of it to become the religious capitol of the Muslims and Christians. Later, printed evidence was released of plans to "Vaticanise the Old City while the Temple Mount is to be declared extra-territorial and handed over to Islam."

A report in April, 1994, revealed that Shimon Peres and Deputy Yossi Beilin concluded a "recognition treaty" with the Holy See. The treaty's secret clauses included giving the Vatican hegemony over the Old City of Jerusalem before the year 2000.

In August, 1994, Mark Halter, a French intellectual and friend of Peres, told the Israeli newspaper *Shishi* that he had delivered a letter from Peres to the Pope outlining plans for Jerusalem. Needless to say, the Palestinian conflict, the Y2K scare, the removal of Peres from leadership and other unexpected events stopped the negotiations cold in their tracks.

According to Halter, Peres offered to hand over sovereignty of Jerusalem's Old City to the Vatican. The city would remain the capital of Israel but would be administered by the Vatican. Jerusalem would have both Israeli and Palestinian mayors, but both would be under orders from the Holy See. The plan was published in an Italian paper three days before Yitzhak Rabin was assassinated.

The Peres plan called for:

- *The extraterritoriality of the Old City and airport at Atarot, which would become a worldwide center.*
- *Jerusalem would become the second Vatican, with all three major religions represented, but under the authority of the Vatican.*
- *The emergence of a Palestinian state in confederation with Jordan with its religious center in East Jerusalem.*
- The Temple Mount would be divided into three regions with then King Hussein overseeing it.

The Vatican has been secretly involved in the peace process between Israel and the Palestinians from the outset. The Peres plan laid out a scenario that fits quite well with Bible Prophecy. A man from the Roman branch of the church will take control of Jerusalem's holiest site and attempt to unite all religions, with help from an Islamic leader.

According to Islamic prophecy, this is the Mahdi, who will, according to Islamic tradition, convert the world to Islam.

The "image of the beast" appears to be an icon created in the form of a person, such as the Antichrist himself. As this image comes alive, the world will gaze in wonder and amazement, believing that Jesus has now returned to earth and is uniting all faiths together. The False Prophet however, will be Christ-less and Cross-less. He is a deceiver who will work under the guise of religion but will be under the influence of Satan himself.

This False Prophet will demand that all people worship the image. Those who refuse will face extermination by beheading (Revelation 20:4). This is a common form of execution in the Muslim faith for those who refuse to follow the strict Islamic law, or are considered blasphemers.

Some well-meaning prophecy teachers identify this image with a huge computer system in Europe. Others teach it is a man-made robot. In this age of modern technology, however, no one is impressed by a giant computer or robot. Certainly no one in this day and age is going to be inspired to worship a giant computer! But people of various religions do worship statues and images. Buddhists burn incense to images, the Hindus' thousands of gods are in the form of images, and the Roman church venerates saints who are often in the form of icons and statues.

The Mary Link

The most interesting link between the Roman Church and the Muslims is not Jesus, but Mary, the mother of Christ.

- *Catholics have a high regard for Mary and many consider her a co-redeemer (which is completely contrary to the New Testament).*
- *Protestants recognize her as a special woman chosen by God for a special mission.*
- *Muslims also have a strong respect for Mary, and her name is mentioned 35 times in the Qur'an. She is referred to as "ever virgin." They teach that Jesus was born of the Virgin Mary.*

Among Muslims, there are two special women—Mary, the mother of Christ, and Fatima, the daughter of Muhammad who is the founder of Islam. The strange link of Mary and Fatima may be the *invisible key* to understanding how these events of prophecy come together.

Many Catholics believe that Muslims will convert to Christianity; but the Muslim teaching is that Christians will eventually convert to Islam. For example, Bishop

Fulton Sheen wrote a book about Mary called *The World's First Love*. In it, he predicted that one day Islam would convert to Christianity—not through Christ but through "a summoning of the Muslims to a veneration of the Mother of God." He wrote:

> *The Qur'an . . . has many passages concerning the Blessed Virgin. First of all, the Qu'ran believes in her Immaculate Conception and also in her Virgin Birth. Mary, then, is for the Muslims the true Sayyida, or Lady. The only possible serious rival to her in their creed would be Fatima, the daughter of Muhammad himself. But after the death of Fatima, Muhammad wrote: "Thou shalt be most blessed of all women in Paradise, after Mary." In a variant of the text, Fatima is made to say, "I surpass all the women, except Mary"* (Fulton J. Sheen, *The World's First Love*. New York: McGraw-Hill, 1952).

Sheen wrote, "Our Lady might be the answer for the crisis between Islam and Christianity." Because of the vision of the three children in Fatima, Portugal, Mary has become known as Our Lady of Fatima. He called her "a pledge and a sign of hope to the Muslim people . . . an assurance that they, who show her so much respect, will one day accept her divine Son too." Speaking of the "special relation between the Virgin Mary and the Muslims," the Roman bishop said:

> *Muslims from various nations, especially from the Middle East, make so many pilgrimages to Our Lady of Fatima's shrine in Portugal that Portuguese officials have expressed concern. The combination of an Islamic name and Islamic devotion to the Blessed*

> *Virgin Mary is a great attraction to Muslims. . . . Fatima is a part of heaven's peace plan.*

On the other hand, Muslims teach that when the Mahdi and Jesus appear, Jesus will command all Christians to deny the Trinity. He will "kill the swine (Jews) and tear down the cross" on the Christian churches. He will then lead a revival, revealing that the only true religion is Islam, and converting the people to Islam.

If Muslims are expecting Christians to convert to Islam and Christians are expecting Muslims to convert to Christianity, then who will convert whom and how will it occur? The link is Mary, and the name is Fatima. We talk about this in the next chapter.

I will tell you the mystery of the woman and of the beast that carries her. . . . Those who dwell on the earth will marvel, whose names are not written in the Book of Life (Revelation 17:7, 8).

7

The Fatima Connection: The Missing Link

In attempting to understand how a possibly defecting pope and a future Islamic leader could merge their followers under one banner, we must understand the common links that could connect the two religions into a future coalition.

When the alleged apparition of Mary appeared to the three children in 1917, it occurred in the village of Fatima, Portugal. The village was named after the daughter of Muhammad, the founder of the Islamic religion. Muhammad was married to numerous wives and had several children during his lifetime. His favorite daughter was named Fatima.

Fatima married her cousin, a man named Ali. When Muhammad passed away, he died rather suddenly and named no specific person to succeed him and continue his religion. As a result, his followers split between two leaders. One group followed Abu Bakr and a second group followed Ali, Muhammad's son-in-law.

The group following Abu Bakr became the Sunni branch and the group following Ali became the Shiite branch. Inner fighting broke out between the two as many of the followers were from various tribes who were already warring before becoming Muslims.

Today, the Sunnis comprise the largest group of Muslims, making up about 80 percent of 1.4 billion Muslims. The second group, the Shiites, consists of about 20 percent and traces its roots to Ali and Fatima. It has been alleged by some that prior to his death, Muhammad whispered a secret into the ear of his daughter, Fatima. I find this interesting for these reasons:

> *When the apparition of Mary appeared to the children in 1917, she became known as "Our Lady of Fatima."*
>
> *The apparition is said to have given a third "secret" to the children. Islamic tradition states that Muhammad revealed a secret to his daughter Fatima.*
>
> *The Fatima apparition alleges that Muslims will convert to Christianity through Mary, not through Christ.*

She Gives Power to the Image

Numerous manuscripts of the New Testament exist today. Although there are no original texts, thousands of quotes found in the writings of the early fathers give us clear proof that those who copied the Scriptures did so with careful accuracy. One of the earliest Bible manuscripts is the Byzantine text, from which much of the King James translation of the Bible came.

When the False Prophet creates the image of the Beast in Revelation 13, the standard English translation of the Bible says, "And he had power to give life unto the image of the beast" (Revelation 13:15).

The *he* in the text refers back to the False Prophet who created the talking image. One of the oldest Greek texts, however, reads, "And *she* gave power to the image of the beast."

When I first read this, years ago in an Interlinear Greek translation of the Bible, I stopped and just looked at the print. I knew I had never seen the word *she* in the English translation. Every other translation I had studied said "he." I began to examine the actual Greek word used in the text, and discovered that it is a *feminine* word and not a masculine one.

Although there is no *she*, or *woman*, mentioned in the entire 13th chapter, there is a *she* elsewhere in the Book of Revelation. John has this woman to represent the false religion that seizes the world during the Tribulation. The imagery is the harlot riding a beast in Revelation 17. The Old Testament pictures religious unfaithfulness as harlotry.

- *The harlot in Revelation 17 is bedecked with gold, precious stones and pearls* (Revelation 17:4).

- *She is drunk with the blood of Christian martyrs and the early saints* (Revelation 17:6).
- *She has a golden chalice in her hand, but it is filled with the abomination and filthiness of her fornication (Revelation 17:4).*
- *She is called "that great city which reigns over the kings of the earth"* (Revelation 17:18).

The *she* in the text could allude to an apostate Roman system that will assist in the creation of this image. After all, most icons are of "saints" or of Christ and His disciples. This would be the first time that a modern, living person (the future Antichrist) would be marked in the form of an icon.

The Apparition in Egypt in 1967

Another possible explanation has an Egyptian connection. There are several reports of apparitions, believed to be of Mary, that have appeared in the Middle East. The most recent and most famous apparition appeared over a Coptic Church in Zeitun, Egypt, near Cairo, from 1967 to 1973. I know two Egyptian Christians in Louisville, Kentucky, who were living in Egypt at the time of this unusual apparition.

One evening a bright light appeared over the top of the church. As people watched, the light morphed into the form of a person. It appeared that doves were flying over the head of the bright image. No words were spoken, but high up, at the top of the church, the image of a person became clear. This was seen by hundreds, not witnessed by one person who attempted to describe it to others.

Each night the apparition appeared over the church and the crowds began to grow. Some suggested it was an angel of the Lord, while others were certain it was Mary appearing as a sign to the Muslims. Some began to report healings occurring, and Egyptian television actually documented the events.

The events were allegedly seen by President Nassar of Egypt who had just experienced a devastating defeat at the hands of the Israelis in the Six-Day War. Throughout Egypt, many were saying this was a sign that the people throughout the Middle East must learn to get along and quit fighting. Author Michael Brown wrote of this event and said:

> *For the first time in Egyptian history, Catholics, Orthodox Christians and Muslims prayed together in public. The Muslims chanted from the Koran, "Mary, God has chosen thee. And purified thee; He has chosen thee above women"* (Michael Brown, *The Final Hour*).

These events indicate that both Catholics and Muslims will join together in certain Middle Eastern Islamic nations when an apparition of Mary, or Our Lady of Fatima, appears. Mary is revered by Catholics and respected by Muslims.

When the statue of our Lady of Fatima is brought out, both Catholics and Muslims bring out their prayer beads. Over 500,000 people of all faiths turned out for two days in Bombay, India, to observe the procession of the statue of Mary. Catholic writers have noted:

> *A Marion revival is spreading throughout Africa, with alleged apparitions of the Virgin Mary, finding a following among Muslims* (*The Tablet*, February 29,1993).

> *African Muslims themselves are seeing apparitions of the Virgin Mary and are not required to become Christians to follow Mary* (*Christian World Report*, 1992).

Please note that Muslims are not required to become Christians to follow Mary. Let us make an assumption. Suppose a bright image in the form of a woman suddenly appeared over the top of the Islamic mosque, the Dome of the Rock, in Jerusalem. What do you think would happen?

I suggest that the apparition would immediately be declared an image of Mary, and people would ascend the Temple Mount by the hundreds. Eventually, thousands would stand in awe of the apparitions. After all, the Marion doctrine has been a central theme received and propagated throughout Europe for centuries.

- *In 1037, King St. Stephen declared Hungary under the protectorate of Mary.*
- *In 1381, Richard II consecrated England to Mary.*
- *In 1638, France was consecrated to Mary by order of King Louis XIII.*
- *In 1650, Poland was given to Mary by King John Casimir.*

- *In 1654, King John IV, the Restorer, consecrated all of Portugal to Mary.*
- *In 1665, Leopold I, who was also the Holy Roman Emperor, gave Austria to Mary.*
- *In 1846, the bishops of America placed themselves under the patronage of the "Holy Mother of God."*

Given the global emphasis on Mary and the Fatima predictions of Muslims being converted to Mary's heart, and the concept that a Muslim can venerate Mary without receiving redemption through Christ, think how these ideas could be used in a future scenario. How could a future False Prophet (perhaps an apostate pope) use these ideas to his advantage?

Project into the future and consider this. The Antichrist has invaded Jerusalem, seizing the Arab section of the Old City which includes the Eastern Gate, the Garden of Gethsemane, the Mount of Olives, the Kidron Valley, the entire Temple Mount and the Western Wall (see Revelation 11:2). He has regained all the land annexed by Israel after the famous Six-Day War of 1967.

As the Islamic world rejoices over the liberation of Jerusalem from Jewish hands, a man who fulfills the Islamic expectations of Isa (Jesus) in Jerusalem, appears alongside the Mahdi (savior) of Islam, the Biblical Antichrist.

This man who appears represents a form of traditional Christianity, but not its doctrine. He tells his followers to create a large image of the new leader of the Middle East and place it on the wing of the Temple area.

On the completion of this image, something occurs to make it "speak and live," as the whole world watches. Muslims accept him as the Jesus of their tradition. There is no need to look for scars in his hands since, according to Muslims, Jesus was never crucified. The miracles are enough to convince them. But what gives power and life to the icon (image)?

Revelation 13:15 says "he" was granted power to give breath to the image, and this freshly-created icon (image) would speak and appear to live. The Greek pronoun in this verse, *autos*, can be translated "he," "she" or "it," according to Strong's Lexicon/ Concordance. It is translated "her" or "she" 195 out of the 236 times it is used in the Bible.

It may be possible that a female apparition will appear over the Temple Mount and capture the attention of the world. If this happens, the freshly-created icon (image) will suddenly be alive and begin to speak.

If this image or icon were to be linked to Mary or Fatima, it would be accepted by the apostate of the Roman church. It would also be accepted by the Islamic followers of their new leader.

It is important to note that any alleged apparition of this type would not be the *real* Mary, the mother of Christ. It would be a counterfeit spirit posing as Mary. I say this because this event will be an "abomination" (Matthew 24:15). It is called the deception where people will "believe a lie . . . [and] be damned" (2 Thessalonians 2:11, 12).

Remember, John saw a future religious system identified by the symbol of a harlot riding a beast (Revelation 17). God gave this warning to His people:

> *And I heard another voice from heaven saying, "Come out of her, my people, lest you share in her sins, and lest you receive of her plagues"* (Revelation 18:4).

The Final Pope

I have spoken to various Catholics about their prophetic beliefs, and many accept the idea that the succession of the popes is coming to a climax as we near the return of Christ. Some suggest there is one more pope after Ratzinger, and others believe two more. Many foresee the Roman church splitting between the faithful and the apostates. Others accept the idea that a future pope will become the false prophet of Revelation 13:11.

If a future pope were to align with the Muslim religion, the headquarters of the new religion would be Jerusalem, the place sacred to both Christians and Muslims. There would be no need for Rome, Italy, and this may be why the city on seven hills, identified as Mystery Babylon in Revelation 17, is burned with fire and destroyed in an hour.

During the seven-year Tribulation, there will be severe persecution against anyone who receives Christ and against Jews in Israel. In fact, many are beheaded and killed for not worshiping the Beast and his image (Revelation 20:4).

The real Mary always pointed people to her Son. The counterfeit Mary spirit will point worship to herself, and not to Christ who is the only redeemer. The ancient world accepted many gods and goddesses in their religions. A revival of goddess worship is presently occurring through the subtle influence of writings and movies such as The Da Vinci Code.

For thus says the Lord: After seventy years are completed at Babylon, I will visit you and perform My good word toward you, and cause you to return to this place (Jeremiah 29:10).

8

The Da Vinci Code and Goddess Worship

When Christ was on earth, the nations around the Mediterranean were steeped in idolatry, worshiping in temples dedicated to many gods of the Roman and Greek religions. Large statues carved from the finest marble were erected in major cities, and beautiful, ornate temples were beehives of activity as worshipers brought sacrifices and gifts.

They paid homage to pagan priests, requesting answers to prayer from gods that could not see or hear. Among the heathen deities were numerous female goddesses, whose followers controlled entire cities in the empire. New Testament apostles discovered the influence of these goddesses when a fortune-telling spirit was cast out of a woman in the city of Philippi. After she lost her power to reveal the future, her "masters" realized their wealth was now gone, so they had Paul and Silas arrested.

Persecution also arose in the city of Ephesus when thousands of worshipers of Diana began burning their occult books and idols in a bonfire (Acts 19:17-19). A man named Demetrius made and sold silver shrines to the townspeople. The revival had converted so many goddess worshipers that now the craftsmen felt threatened by Paul, who was preaching that the true God was not created with human hands.

As the early church continued to reach into pagan nations, the influence of the gospel began replacing the influence of the gods and goddesses of the Empire. There was however, severe persecution against Christians for their total commitment to one God—Jesus Christ.

This persecution ensued for centuries, costing the lives of hundreds of thousands of believers throughout the Roman Empire. Eventually, Emperor Constantine rose to power and made Christianity the official religion of the Roman Empire. During these times, another "woman" began replacing the many female deities scattered across the Empire. That woman was Mary.

The Da Vinci Code

Recently, interest in a woman being the original leader of the early Christian church was renewed in a book called *The Da Vinci Code,* by author Dan Brown.

Using Italian artist Leonardo Da Vinci's "The Last Supper" as a device, Brown lays out a huge conspiracy theory, alleging that the person with red hair to the right of Jesus in the painting is actually Mary Magdalene.

Brown's imagination runs wild as he sees a person who seems to have small breasts. His clothes and those of Jesus seem to be the reverse of each other. He states that there appears to be the form of a vee (V) between Jesus and this disciple; which, Brown alleges, was an ancient female symbol. Brown then imagines that Peter is facing him with a "disembodied hand" wielding a dagger, as if Peter is ready to lunge and kill Mary.

With his own interpretation as his guide, Brown then embellishes history and facts, defiantly twisting both, along with Scriptures, to teach that Jesus and Mary Magadalene were actually secretly married and Mary had a child by Jesus. According to Brown, Mary was actually given control of the Christian church, but spiritual authority was wrested from her by Peter.

Brown's conspiracy theory has Mary fleeing to France where she gave birth to a daughter and was protected by Jews. This only daughter eventually married and produced a special bloodline. Eventually, this bloodline intermarried with the French Royal bloodline throughout the centuries.

The bloodline, known as the Merovingian bloodline, produced the kings and leaders of Europe for centuries. Eventually, a group formed the famed Knights Templar. Founded in 1099 by the French King, Godfrey of Bouillon, the Knights allegedly traveled to Jerusalem and discovered secret documents under the Temple Mount.

The legend continues as eventually the Knights were killed by Pope Clement V and Phillip IV of France and the secret documents fell into the hands of the Priory of Zion. Brown attempts to use numerous historical "facts" to confirm his conspiracy theory.

Knowledgeable scholars who have thoroughly researched Brown's claims have debunked many parts of his theory as legend, twisted history and outright fantasy.

The bottom line is, according to Brown, Jesus made no claims to deity and through his secret marriage to Mary, Jesus has a physical bloodline on earth. The thesis announces that the Catholic Church for centuries has tried to hide this secret, and by originally forcing the church out of Mary Magdalene's hands and giving it to Peter (the first pope) they have hidden the truth from the masses.

Without going into a lot of detail, three Gnostic gospels speak of Mary Magdalene: the *Gospel of Truth*, the *Gospel of Thomas* and the *Gospel of Philip*. Not one of the three says anything about Jesus marrying anyone, including Mary Magdalene. The Bible doesn't, either. Brown claims that the Gospel of Phillip, written in Aramaic, says that Mary was Jesus' *companion*, which in Aramaic means "spouse."

First, the Gospel of Phillip was not written in Aramaic but in Coptic. Scholars agree that there is not an

Aramaic or Hebrew word for companion that means "spouse." The word *companion* is used in the Old and New Testaments for "a friend or a companion," when speaking of people!

Brown surmises that "Jesus being a married man makes infinitely more sense than our standard Biblical views of Jesus, because the social decorum during that time virtually forbade a Jewish man to be unmarried" (page 245). Again, this is incorrect. In Matthew 19:12, Jesus spoke of unmarried men who were called *eunuchs*. He said:

> *There are eunuchs who were born thus from their mother's womb, and there are eunuchs who were made eunuchs by men, and there are eunuchs who have made themselves eunuchs for the kingdom of heaven's sake.*

The apostle Paul stated in 1 Corinthians 7:8 that he was unmarried. Paul even taught that believers should attempt to discipline themselves and remain unmarried to do God's work more effectively. Paul also taught that some have a gift of celibacy and others do not (1 Corinthians 7:7).

The reason Christ never obtained earthly wealth or built an earthly empire is because He knew He would not remain on earth forever. He never married because His "bride" is the church and His family is the sons and daughters birthed into the Kingdom of God by being born again of the water and the Spirit. Christ remains faithful to one bride, His church, and not a physical woman he met during His life on earth.

The Inherent Danger of This Theory

The danger of such a book as *The Da Vinci Code* is that people will accept what they read as fact without researching the information. Consider this:

- *Americans love a conspiracy theory, and many have been advanced since the 9/11 attacks and the beginning of the war in Iraq.*
- *About 40 percent of the women who have read the Da Vinci Code believe it is accurate, including numerous Christian women.*
- *In several recent instances, young people have quit church and turned from the faith after reading this book. They have lost confidence in the local church and in the faith of their forefathers.*

Brown's theory implies that the first century church was actually based on the "female goddess" principle. Once again we are seeing a revival of the female goddess religion in these last days. The spread of this concept throughout the world is important, when we consider the prophetic ramifications of it.

The old Roman, Greek and Babylonian Empires were once filled with idolatry, including the worship of numerous gods and goddesses. Most Evangelical prophetic teachers see the European Union (EU) as a reviving of the ancient Roman Empire territory.

This reviving means borderless countries, a single currency, a leader overseeing the unity and, eventually, a united form of religion. Presently, the Catholic Church is the predominant religion throughout most of Europe.

No offense is intended to sincere God-fearing Catholics, but many in Europe accept Mary, the mother of Jesus, as more than His mother. They recognize her as the "mother of God" and as a co-redeemer, meaning that there is salvation through Mary *and* through Christ! This is another form of the "goddess worship" found in the ancient Roman Empire.

When Mary was pregnant with Jesus, she said, "My soul magnifies the Lord, and my spirit has rejoiced in God my Savior" (Luke 1:46, 47).

Once, a woman attempted to exalt Mary in the presence of Jesus by saying, "Blessed is the womb that bore You, and the breasts which nursed You" (Luke 11:27). At that moment, Jesus did not exalt Mary or brag on her. Instead, Jesus said to them:

> *More than that, blessed are those who hear the word of God and keep it* (Luke 11:28).

Mary was present in the Upper Room when Christ told his followers to tarry in Jerusalem for the promise of the Holy Spirit (Luke 24:49; Acts 1:4; 14). Luke calls her "Mary, the mother of Jesus," not "Mary, the mother of God" (Acts 1:14). This is because God has no beginning or end, and Christ pre-existed with God before His physical birth on earth (John 1:1-14).

God has no mother, and neither did the pre-incarnate Christ. God *formed* a body in the womb of Mary, and Christ the eternal Word of God entered that created body (Hebrews 10:5). Many in the Roman church are convinced that Mary is co-equal with Christ.

Yet, the *Encyclopedia Britannica* says, "During the first centuries of the church, there was no emphasis on Mary." The *Catholic Encyclopedia* points out, "There is no ground for surprise if we do not meet with any clear traces of the cultus of the Blessed Virgin Mary in the first Christian centuries."

In 1869, Johann Joseph Döllinger wrote in *The Pope and the Council*:

> *Neither the New Testament, nor the Patristic writings tell us anything about the destiny of the Holy Virgin after the death of Christ. Two apocryphal works of the fourth and fifth centuries are the earliest suggestions about her assumption* (pp. 28, 29).

Where and how did Mary receive all of the attention in our contemporary time? The answer may surprise you.

Maia, the Greek Goddess

Early Greek mythology tells of a goddess named Maia, who consorted with Zeus and produced a son named Hermes. The month of May is named after Maia, who became known as the "Queen of May."

In the Old Testament, a "queen of heaven" was being worshiped hundreds of years before the title, Queen of Heaven, was given to Mary. In Jeremiah's day, women burned incense and baked cakes to this "Queen of heaven."

Bible scholars say this idol goddess was related in some way to a Persian and Assyrian deity who was supposed to symbolize a quality possessed by the moonlight, giving its receptive power to nature. The symbol of this goddess was a crescent moon over her head. The moon thus became generally the symbol of female productiveness, and was worshiped as such at Babylon.

Jeremiah mentions the idolatrous worship of the "queen of heaven" five times, and revealed that God was judging the nation of Israel for the sin of worshiping this heavenly queen (Jeremiah 7:18; 44:17; 18; 19; 25).

> *The children gather wood, the fathers kindle the fire, and the women knead dough, to make cakes for the queen of heaven; and they pour out drink offerings to other gods, that they may provoke Me to anger* (Jeremiah 7:18).

Mary and Ephesus

Most Roman Catholics cheerfully refer to the Virgin Mary as the Queen of Heaven, and understand this to be a term of endearment, love and adoration. *Time* magazine said:

> *Among all women who have ever lived, the mother of Jesus is the most celebrated and the most venerated. . . . Among Roman Catholics, the Madonna is recognized not only as the Mother of God, but, according to modern Popes, as the Queen of the Universe, Queen of Heaven, Seat of Wisdom, and even the Spouse of the Holy Spirit* (*Time* Magazine, "Handmaid or Feminist?" December 30, 1991. pp. 62, 66).

By the time Constantine became Emperor of Rome and legalized Christianity, there was a keen interest in converting the heathen to the Christian church. In their zeal, they began mixing pagan holidays and beliefs with the Christian faith. Numerous heathens in the third and fourth centuries worshiped goddesses in their temples, so it became apparent that Mary could be the replacement to fill in the gap.

Historically, Mary worship was initiated in Ephesus. A synodal letter of the Council of Ephesus indicates that John took Mary with him to Ephesus, where she eventually died in A.D. 63.

Later, it was taught that she lived and died in Jerusalem and was buried in Gethsemane. A legend developed that Thomas went to open her grave, but her body was gone and only a fragrance was left. This theory is impossible, however, since Thomas became a missionary and was martyred thousands of miles away in India!

Ramsey MacMullen, Dunham Professor of History and Classics at Yale University, is considered by many to be the greatest historian of the Roman Empire. His book, *Christianizing the Roman Empire: AD 100-400*, reveals some amazing information he found in his research.

In Acts 19, Paul preached a great revival in Ephesus that broke the occult powers controlling the city. John the apostle eventually moved to Ephesus with Mary, the mother of Jesus. According to MacMullen's research, John eventually entered the famous Temple of Diana, the chief female goddess of the entire area. While John was praying, the altar in the temple split down the middle, causing half of the temple to fall. This act of judgment brought a revival to Ephesus, and within 50 years hardly anyone was worshiping Diana.

For 200 years, Ephesus was the center of the Christian faith. Eventually, under Constantine, Christianity was moved from Ephesus to Rome, and eventually controlled by the Roman church. It was about this time that Mary began to be called, “The mother of God.”

In A.D. 431, the Council of Ephesus was convened, and declared Mary to be the “mother of God.” It was also at this time that a shrine, or idol, of Mary was constructed *with a crescent moon over her head*! Thus the concepts of Mary, the Mother of God, and Mary, the Queen of Heaven, were combined and venerated in the Roman church.

In early history, the women of Thrace and Arabia made cakes and burned them for Mary. The Bishop Epiphanius rebuked these women for this. Yet, over time, the doctrine of Mariology began to take a foothold in the Catholic belief. Here are some expressions of this doctrine:

- *Saint Germanus wrote, "There is no one, O most holy Mary who can be saved or redeemed but through thee."*
- *Saint Bernard wrote, "As we have access to the Eternal Father only through Jesus Christ, so have we access to Jesus Christ only through Mary."*

- *He also said, "All men, past and present, to come should look to Mary as the means and negotiator of salvation. By thee we have access to the Son, Mother of salvation."*

I must boldly say that the Bible totally contradicts these theories. John wrote:

> *He who believes in the Son has everlasting life* (John 5:24).

Luke recorded, "Believe on the Lord Jesus Christ, and you will be saved" (Acts 16:31). The apostle Paul penned these words, "In [Christ] we have redemption through his blood" (Colossians 1:14). Peter added, "Nor is there salvation in any other, for there is no other name under heaven given among men by which we must be saved" (Acts 4:12).

In 1854, almost 1,800 years after Mary's death, Pope Pius IX announced that all the church should accept the doctrine of the Immaculate Conception, the belief that Mary was free from any original sin the moment of her conception. This teaching would imply that two people were free from sin from the moment of conception, Jesus and Mary.

The Roman church had taught for many years that at the very end of her life, Mary was caught up into heaven alive, prior to her death. On November 1, 1950, Pope Pius XII declared "infallibly" that the "Assumption" of Mary was a dogma of the Catholic faith.

Throughout its long history, it seems, whenever the Bible and Roman church tradition conflict, man-made traditions win out. Yet, we must rely on the Scriptures, not tradition, or it is possible to be deceived.

A Woman Riding a Beast

In Revelation 17, the apostle John saw an astonishing vision of a woman riding a beast. This woman represents the final religious system that will be destroyed prior to the return of Christ to Jerusalem. Why is this system identified with a woman (a harlot) on a beast, and not a man on a beast?

In Scripture, harlotry stands for:

- ❏ *false gods* (Micah 1:7),
- ❏ *false worship* (Ezekiel 16), and
- ❏ *false devotion* (Hosea 2:5).

A spiritual harlot represents a false religious system (Jeremiah 3:1, 6 8).

First, the image of a woman on a beast is linked to an ancient legend of how Europe came into existence. The legend says a woman sat on a beast on a "city on seven hills." Two major prophetic cities were built on seven hills—Rome in Italy and Constantinople in Turkey (Istanbul today).

According to *The Catholic Encyclopedia*, "It is within the city of Rome, called the city of seven hills, that the entire area of the Vatican State proper is now confined." An ancient coin was minted showing a woman sitting on seven hills. This woman is the goddess Europa, from which the name Europe was derived.

In ancient mythology, *Europa* became a female goddess who rode on a bull with crescent horns, the symbol in the Middle East for Baal. The bull was Zeus, the father of the gods in disguise; and Baal was the ruling god of ancient Babylon.

As the two plunged into the Mediterranean, they rode through the sea from Pheonicia (now Lebanon) to Crete, with the woman clinging to the bull's horns for strength and power.

On reaching the shore, Zeus returned to his original form and gave all the land to the north of Crete to Europa. In many places throughout Europe today, there are large statues of a woman (Europa) clinging to the horns of a bull.

This Greek myth was well-known thoughout Asia and the Middle East at the time John penned the Book of Revelation. When he said he saw a "woman riding a beast," many in his time would have immediately thought of the Greek myth.

John was not promoting a myth, however, but was revealing a clue, through symbolism, about the link of this woman to a future religious system in Europe and the Middle East.

In Revelation 17, the woman is on a beast with 10 horns. These 10 horns are 10 major nations with 10 kings, forming a coalition with the future Antichrist. The beast is scarlet in color. The woman is decked in gold and jewels. She holds a gold cup in her hand. The meaning can be two-fold.

One, since these 10 nations include parts of Europe and the Middle East, the woman can allude to the area of the world in which she rides, namely the area of the old Roman Empire and Europe.

Two, the woman is identified as a harlot, or an idolatrous religious system. Oddly, the identification of this woman is similar in many ways to the items and colors found in the liturgy of a Roman church.

Just as the Virgin Mary gave birth to the Son of God, Jesus Christ, the woman on the beast is a picture of an impure religious system that gives birth to the False Prophet. He will pose as Christ, and perform satanic miracles to deceive the nations.

The prophecy itself gives the vital clue that leads us to the true identification of the woman:

> *And the woman whom you saw is that great city which reigns over the kings of the earth* (Revelation 17:18).

In John's day this was understood as Rome. John himself saw the destruction of Rome, and he could not, and would not, have written about it in plain language. A sure way to instant death would have been to announce that "Rome will be destroyed." John was already banished to the Isle of Patmos as a political prisoner.

This is why God veiled the identity of this woman in symbolism, calling her "Mystery Babylon." In Jewish teaching, the ancients understood the word *Babylon* to be a code word for Rome. There were many reasons for this, and here are just a few:

- ❑ *Both Rome and Babylon invaded Israel,*
- ❑ *Both razed the Temple on the 9th of Av,*
- ❑ *Both burned the city of Jerusalem, and*
- ❑ *Both took Jews away as captive slaves.*

The coding of Rome as Babylon is also seen in the *Apocalypse of Ezra* (4 Ezra and 2 Ezra 3-14), in *2 Baruch* (or the *Second Apocalypse of Baruch*), and the *Sybyine Oracles*. These are all well-known Jewish pseudepigrapha texts.

Catholic writer Karl Keating identifies the Babylon mentioned in 1 Peter 5:13, as Rome. As late as A.D. 303, the early father, Eusebius, stated that Rome was Babylon.

The woman acquired her kingdom from the kings of the earth. In John's day, the Roman Empire ruled from its political center in Rome, Italy. Eventually political Rome was mingled with the religious systems of Rome under Constantine.

Today, the Roman church is a leading power player in Europe and in parts of the Middle East. The Pope can still retain the respect of the traditional Christian faiths *and* the Muslims when he travels in countries controlled by Muslim governments.

John gives the amazing scenario that the woman (Rome) will be destroyed in an hour by the leaders of the very beast she rides on. Why would the 10 kings destroy the city of Rome? While this is more speculation than prophetic insight, if a false pope arises, as some teach, and follows the Antichrist to Jerusalem, then Jerusalem, not Rome, would be the center of the new global religion.

I believe that the Antichrist will be from an Islamic background. If this is true, there is no logic or need for his headquarters to be centered in Rome, since the city has been marked by the "Christian religion" for centuries. Jerusalem, however, is the third most sacred site for Muslims and the second most important site for the Roman church.

With the spread of such fallacies and legends as the Da Vinci Code and the mind-set of many throughout Europe and the Middle East, it is easy to see how the Roman concept of Mary would fit into a new "world" religion. What are the common links between Roman Christians and Muslims?

- ❑ *Christians believe in the inspired 66 Books of the Bible, while the Muslims accept the Torah, the Psalms and the four Gospels, but believe the verses have been changed to accommodate the doctrines of the Jews and Christians.*
- ❑ *Both believe in the same God in concept, but use different names.*
- ❑ *Both have a belief in Jesus. Christians, however, believe He was God's son, crucified for our sins, and raised from the dead. Muslims deny that Christ was God's Son and do not believe He was crucified.*

They believe He will return, but not to bring peace to the world:

> *Jesus, the son of Mary, will descend at the end of time and judge among the people with justice, following the law of our prophet Muhammad. He will break the crosses and kill the swine . . . He will only accept Islam from the people* (Answers to Common Questions from New Muslims).

The common link, therefore, is not Jesus. The most common link between the Roman church and the Muslims is Mary.

The people of the prince who is to come shall destroy the city and the sanctuary. The end of it shall be with a flood, and til the end of the war desolations are determined (Daniel 9:26).

9

The Temple Link to the War over Jerusalem

Jerusalem will be ground zero for the final end-time conflict. Prophecy scholars and observers of the times clearly see that radical Islamic organizations are casting their eyes on Jerusalem. To believers in the Islamic religion, the sacred city is the third holiest piece of real estate on the planet.

Since the seventh century, the famous Islamic mosques, El Aqsa and the golden Dome of the Rock, have towered over the center of the Jewish Temple Mount. The mosque complex serves as a reminder that Jews and Christians have no spiritual, legal or political control of the Temple Mountain.

Prior to Israel's reestablishment as a nation in 1948, it was generally understood in the Islamic world that the Temple Mount once housed the Temple of Solomon and the Temple of Herod, and that it was once the Jewish mountain of worship.

In recent times a Muslim, Khaleel Muhammad, Assistant Professor of Religious Studies at San Diego State University, has pointed out the fact the Qu'ran actually teaches that Jerusalem belongs to the Jews.

According to Professor Mohammad, the Qur'an says more about Moses than about any other person. He refers to God's warning to Israel through Moses by quoting in the Qu'ran, Sura 5:20, 21:

> *Moses said to his people: O my people! Remember the bounty of God upon you when He bestowed prophets upon you, and made you kings and gave you that which had not been given to anyone before you amongst the nations. O my people! Enter the Holy Land which God has written for you, and do not turn tail, otherwise you will be losers.*

The professor stated that the Qu'ran actually says the term *Holy Land* was "written for the Israelites." In both Jewish and Islamic understanding, the term alludes to "a finality, decisiveness and immutability." He pointed out that the medieval scholars "without any exception known to me," interpreted the words of the Qu'ran to acknowledge that Israel belonged to the Jews.

Mohammad says the idea that Israel does not belong to the Jews is a modern belief. Muslims around the world are taught that Jerusalem is mentioned in the Qu'ran as the site where Mohammad took his famous night journey, from the "furtherest mosque," on his white horse. I have visited inside the Dome of the Rock and was told to place my hand inside a man-made box and I would "feel" the footprint Muhammad's horse made when he ascended from the rock to return to Medina.

This tradition was challenged by Ahmed Mahmad Oufa, a Muslim commentator in the official Egyptian government weekly, the *Al-Ahram Weekly*!

Oufa stated that the entire claim of the night journey being from Jerusalem at the location of the Al-Aqsa mosque is based on a mistaken reading of one chapter in the Qur'an and one verse that mentions the night journey. According to Oufa, the verse actually alludes to a mosque near the city of Mecca in Arabia, and not in Jerusalem.

The verse in question reads that Muhammad was brought at night from one mosque to "the furthest mosque"—*aqsa* in Arabic. Early Islamic commentators didn't associate this with Jerusalem until the 8th century, when Muslims felt they had to give some type of sanctity to Jerusalem.

From the beginning of Islam, they had understood the Temple Mount as being sacred because of the two Jewish Temples that were once there. It should be noted that the Qu'ran could not be talking about Jerusalem, since Al Aqsa was built in the year 715, nearly a hundred years after the death of Muhammad!

Why Was the Dome Built?

If the center of Islam was in Arabia, why would Muslims be interested in building a major mosque in Jerusalem? Important scientific research conducted by Ya'akov Ofir has revealed some very interesting details about the origin of the Muslim Dome of the Rock, located on the Mosque compound. His findings show that it was commissioned by Islamic Caliph Abd el-Malik, in A.D. 691, for the Jews as their "last house" of prayer. El-Malik, was the Umayyad ruler of Damascus who also controled the land of Israel in those days. Ofir's findings reveal the following:

- ❑ *The Dome of the Rock was never built as a mosque.*
- ❑ *It does not resemble a typical mosque.*
- ❑ *It was never used as a mosque until 1947.*
- ❑ *No mosque anywhere in the world looks like it.*
- ❑ *The Dome of the Rock was not built facing Mecca. It is in the shape of an octagon, with its points corresponding to the points of the compass.*
- ❑ *In 1947, Haj Amim al Husseini, the Nazi Muslim who supported Hitler and uncle of Yassar Arafat, declared the Dome of the Rock to be a mosque.*

The odd, eight-sided Dome of the Rock was originally patterned after a fourth century Christian shrine sitting on the Mount of Olives. It had been erected to recognize the Ascension of Jesus to heaven. Some scholars believe it was deliberately built as a counter-attraction to the two mosques in Mecca and Medina.

Because of a religious-political conflict in Islam, those two cities were under the control of a rival caliph.

As a result the Caliph of Jerusalem built the shrine for Jews and began to emphasize the importance of Muslims making a pilgrimage to Jerusalem to see the place where Muhammad made his "night journey."

Today, the Temple Mount in Jerusalem is surrounded by non–Muslims. The old city is divided into the Jewish, Christian and Muslim sections of Jerusalem. The fact that one of their holiest sites is surrounded by the "infidel" Christians and Jews is a slap in the face of their religious beliefs for many strict Muslims.

The so called "Palestinian Conflict" is propagated as a struggle to give up land for peace. First, it was the Gaza Strip, then the so-called West Bank, consisting of Judea and Samaria. Eventually, it will be Jerusalem. The Muslims' ultimate goal is to remove the Christian and Jewish presence completely from eastern Jerusalem and from Israel itself.

When the Jewish Temple Is Reconstructed

Daniel 9:17 says that the Temple in Jerusalem will become desolate. When the "abominations" make Jerusalem desolate, this will occur on the "wing of the Temple" (Daniel 9:27; 11:31). The New Testament contains same rather cryptic references to a future Temple on the Temple Mount in Jerusalem.

In Matthew 24:15, 21, Matthew spoke of this occurring during the "great tribulation."

According to Jesus, people will see with their own eyes "the 'abomination of desolation,' spoken of by Daniel the prophet, standing in the holy place" (Matthew 24:15). Paul wrote that the "man of sin" (the Antichrist) "sits as God in the temple of God, showing himself that he is God" (2 Thessalonians 2:4).

In the Book of Revelation, the last Book of the Bible, John recorded—25 years after the destruction of the Jewish Temple in Jerusalem—that he was to:

> *[M]easure the temple of God, the altar, and those who worship there. But leave out the court which is outside the temple, and do not measure it, for it has been given to the Gentiles. And they will tread the holy city underfoot for forty-two months* (Revelation 11:1, 2).

Some suggest that the Revelation passage was penned prior to A.D. 70, *before* the destruction of the Jewish Temple by the Romans. Others teach that John is measuring the Temple of God in heaven, but this is totally inaccurate for how could the Gentiles trample the Holy City in heaven for 42 months?

The future Temple will be constructed in Jerusalem on the Temple Mount. Most Christians are unaware of organizations in Israel that are researching the Bible, history and archeology. They are making replicas of the Temple furniture, organizing names for future Priests and Levites, and studying ancient Temple rituals.

The conflict of an Islamic mosque and a Jewish Temple being built on the same mountain is utterly unthinkable. Since the "outer court is given to the Gentiles," however, it is possible the Jewish Temple could be constructed north of the Dome of the Rock, with hundreds of feet separating the two facilities.

The Invasion of Jerusalem

The Jewish Temple will be rebuilt by Hebrew people during the first 42 months of the Tribulation. According to Mike Coleman who met with a Hebrew Scholar from the Hebrew University, if the Jews started building a future Temple, it would be 42 months before the dedication could occur. This is because certain prayers must be prayed on the Sabbath, Feast Days and New Moons, in accordance with the Law and Jewish traditions.

This scenario fits well if we consider the Antichrist invades Jerusalem in the middle of the Tribulation, or after the first 42 months. It may also be why the Bible indicates that the Antichrist will "bring an end to sacrifice and offering" (Daniel 9:27).

This invasion may occur around the time of Passover, when the possible Temple dedication would occur. If the Antichrist, working in co-operation with the Palestinian people and the many-splintered Islamic groups, seized total control of East Jerusalem and the Temple Mount from any form of Jewish presence, he would be referred to and hailed as a modern hero.

The Antichrist will slay the two witnesses, one of whom is Elijah (Malachi 4:5). The death of these two prophets will release joy to the world, and men will send gifts to one another in celebration (Revelation 11:10).

The dead bodies of these two men will remain on the street for three and a half days (Revelation 11:11). After 84 hours, God will raise them from the dead and they will ascend into heaven. This will cause great fear in men, and a sudden earthquake will kill 7,000 people in Jerusalem (Revelation 11:12, 13).

This will divert attention from the Antichrist, but the distraction is short-lived as the False Prophet joins the man of sin in Jerusalem and builds an image that will speak and live. Those who reject worship of the Beast will be killed by beheading, the Islamic method of execution for certain crimes and for infidels who reject Islam at that time (Revelation 13:15; 20:4).

The rise of the False Prophet will bring a final death sentence to the city of seven hills—Rome, Italy—that has ruled over the kings of the earth (Revelation 17:18). Identified in symbolism as "Mystery Babylon," the city which for over 2,000 years produced the Caesars, the military legions and the Popes of the Holy Roman Empire, will cease to exist in an hour's time (Revelation 18:17).

Thus, the last vestige of historic Christianity is removed from the earth as the Jews are assaulted in Israel and are fleeing the city for their own protection (Revelation 12).

The False Prophet will possibly pose as Christ. He will attempt to authenticate this claim by the miracles of calling fire down from heaven and causing the image of the beast to speak and live.

The world's population will be so far removed from the truth of God's Word that "because they did not receive the love of the truth," they will believe a lie and be condemned (2 Thessalonians 2:11).

The False Prophet can fulfill the Islamic belief that Isa (Jesus) will appear in Jerusalem in the future.

The missing link that can connect these two religions could very well be an apparition of Mary, linked to the name Fatima. A ghostly apparition over the Temple Mount, coupled with fire coming from heaven and a speaking icon, is a combination that would sweep millions into a major religious deception. The Bible warns that even the elect could be deceived by what is coming (Matthew 24:24).

The Islamic Jesus will deny the Trinity and proclaim he is not the son of God. According to John's epistle, this is the spirit of Antichrist!

> *Who is a liar but he who denies that Jesus is the Christ? He is antichrist who denies the Father and the Son* (1 John 2:22).
>
> *And every spirit that does not confess that Jesus Christ has come in the flesh is not of God. And this is the spirit of the Antichrist, which you have heard was coming, and is now already in the world* (1 John 4:3).

For many deceivers have gone out into the world who do not confess Jesus Christ as coming in the flesh. This is a deceiver and an antichrist (2 John 7).

The Roman Link

History reveals that for centuries the Roman church has been the strongest spiritual–political force in Europe. The critical role it has played in the history of that continent has made it a world leader out of proportion to its physical size.

A tangled network of evolving politics and a growing trend toward increased political unity make Europe an important partner in the drama of end-time events. The Roman church is the key player in this scenario!

The thing that makes this all seem impossible is Islam. Add to the above scene a growing revival of Islam, its hatred of anything Jewish or Western, and the rapidly increasing attraction of some of its devotees to terrorism and you have a volatile mix.

Some are saying there can never be an accommodation of Christianity and Islam on the political spectrum.

God's word of prophecy is unerring, however. He knows the future as well as He knows the past. What He has said through His prophets and His Word will come to pass:

[God] changes the times and the seasons; He removes kings and raises up kings; He gives wisdom

to the wise and knowledge to those who have understanding. He reveals deep and secret things; He knows what is in the darkness (Daniel 2:21, 22).

In this book you have seen how events in history have come together to set the stage for these last days. Visions of Fatima and ancient prophecies of certain popes have eerily predicted some of the things we are seeing today.

You have seen how God used Pope John Paul II, President Reagan and Mikhail Gorbachev to shape history and create the conditions for the events of Revelation.

Europe's record of history, its geography and its culture merely enhance the prophetic role of the two religions in Scripture.

This reminds believers that we are nearing the return of the Lord Jesus Christ. The harvest is being reaped in a greater way than ever before. Yet, we have less time than we have ever had. We must increase our efforts to win the lost for Christ.

Concluding Thoughts

The prophetic Scriptures lay down certain definite facts about the future:

1. A Great Tribulation is coming at the end of the age (Matthew 24:21).

2. A man identified as the Antichrist will rise on the scene (Revelation 13:1, 2).

3. A religious leader, a false prophet, will follow the Antichrist (Revelation 13:11).

4. The false prophet will build an image of the beast, the Antichrist (Revelation 13:14).

5. The false prophet will make the image speak and live (Revelation 13:15).

6. Those who do not worship the image will be beheaded (Revelation 20:4).

In this prophetic study, I have attempted to tie the pieces of the puzzle together and paint a possible scenario of how events will unfold, and what could occur to bring about the final deception of the last days. We know there will be counterfeit miracles that will deceive those who love not the truth.

> *Only He who now restrains will do so until He is taken out of the way. And then the lawless one will be revealed, whom the Lord will consume with the breath of His mouth and destroy with the brightness of His coming. The coming of the lawless one is according to the working of Satan, with all power, signs, and lying wonders, and with all unrighteous deception among those who perish, because they did not receive the love of the truth, that they might be saved* (2 Thessalonians 2:7-10).

Since the important future political and religious activity will center around the Mediterranean area, the Roman Church and Islamic leaders must come to some form of agreement. For this to occur, the Roman leader must be an apostate pope who denies the deity of Christ.

The false prophet will apear as Jesus, the Messiah, and deceive multitudes in the Islamic religion. They will falsely believe that Isa (Jesus) has once again appeared on earth to fulfill their prophecies that He will "deny the Trinity, kill the swine (the Jews), and tear down the crosses," or defeat Christianity. Counterfeit miracles will help to authenticate and reenforce the deception that Christ has returned.

As I have outlined in this book, the main link between the Roman Church and Islam is the concept and veneration of Mary.

I believe it is possible, even probable, that a false apparition will be central in pulling these two diverse groups together and initiating the great delusion Paul warned of in 2 Thessalonians. Remember, when the Bible mentions deception and delusion, it alludes to a religious deception, not a political or social one.

The majority of wars occurring in the world in the 21st century are being initiated by a new breed of Islamic fanatics who are bent on taking over the world and forcing people to convert to Islam. This is happening in Africa, in the Middle East, and in certain Asian nations.

According to Scripture, the cry in the last days will be for peace. Paul warned, however:

> *When they say, "Peace and safety!" then sudden destruction comes upon them, as labor pains upon a pregnant woman. And they shall not escape* (1 Thessalonians 5:3).

In modern times, the Roman church has emphasized peace throughout the world. Islamic peace is not peace as the Western world recognizes it. Peace to fanatic Muslims means if you obey all the laws of Islam and pay the Islamic tax, you will not be harassed or killed.

Time will be the interpreter of all prophetic Scripture. As Paul said, "For now we see through a glass, darkly," and we "we know in part, and we prophesy in part" (1 Corinthians 13:9, 12). I have attempted through inspiration and research, to paint a picture of how certain events will unfold in the future. Of course only the Holy Spirit knows the vivid and clear details of all future events.

There must be a link that pulls the two main religions under one man in Jerusalem. If the false prophet poses as Christ, and the Antichrist works against the true Christ (Jesus) and receives the Islamic version of Christ (the false prophet), then the only link would be an apostate pope who uses the concept of Mary and Fatima to pull the religions under a single banner. A false miracle will be the "sign" to them that he is the real Jesus.

I emphasize that this Mary will not be the blessed virgin who carried the body of Christ in her womb, and the blessed woman who followed her Son to the cross. It will be a counterfeit spirit whose worship of the image of the beast will lead multitudes into perdition.

Jesus warned of deceptions, and Paul warned of lying signs and wonders. Keep your eyes on the Author and Finisher of your faith, and you will never be led astray by any future end-time deception.

How To Be Saved

Step 1: Realize that you are a sinner and for your soul to be saved, you need to come to God.

God created us to have a relationship with Him. He wants us to experience true and lasting peace in this life. Blaise Pascal, the French philosopher and mathematician, said, "There is a God-shaped vacuum in the heart of every man which cannot be filled by any created thing, but only by God, the Creator, made known through Jesus."

The Bible confirms what we already know: "All have sinned and fall short of the glory of God" (Romans 3:23). This is why the peace of God eludes you in your vain search for reality: "Your iniquities have separated you from your God; and your sins have hidden His face from you" (Isaiah 59:2). Reality is knowing Him!

Step 2: Acknowledge the fact that you cannot save yourself.

> *There is a way that seems right to a man, but its end is the way of death* (Proverbs 14:12).

Nothing works. Regardless of which path you choose, it seems, the peace of God eludes you. Your own attempts to solve your problems have ended in disaster.

You have tried good works and found your efforts to be meaningless, empty, without Christ. Riches cannot buy salvation. Fame or good breeding does not impress God. Personal suffering cannot save. Yet, you realize you desperately need the touch of God in your life!

Step 3: Believe that Jesus Christ can and will save you!

> *Jesus said . . , "I am the way, the truth, and the life. No one comes to the Father except through Me"* (John 14:6).
>
> *The one who comes to Me I will by no means cast out* (John 6:37).

Jesus Christ died on the cross and rose from the dead to pay the penalty for our sin and restore our lost relationship with God.

Step 4: Confess your sins to God and accept Jesus Christ as your Savior.

> *Here I am! I stand at the door and knock. If anyone hears my voice and opens the door, I will come in and eat with him, and he with me* (Revelation 3:20, NIV).
>
> *If you confess with your mouth the Lord Jesus and believe in your heart that God has raised Him from the dead, you will be saved. For with the heart one believes unto righteousness, and with the mouth confession is made unto salvation. For "whoever calls on the name of the Lord shall be saved"* (Romans 10:9, 10, 13).

You can receive Jesus Christ into your heart right now. Wherever you are, whoever you are, whatever you have done in the past, He will gladly come to your spirit and give you peace. His free gift of salvation is your only hope to find the answer to your lifelong quest for meaning and true happiness. He awaits your decision. Will you sincerely pray this sinner's prayer with me?

Dear Lord Jesus, I acknowledge that I am a sinner and need your forgiveness. I believe You died for my sins. I want to turn from my sins and give You my heart. I repent of my sins and invite you to come into my life. I now trust you as Savior, and make you Lord of my life. In Jesus' name. Amen.

If you prayed this prayer sincerely, and you believe God has heard, you are saved! We believe with our hearts, then we tell others what God has done for us.

It is important to me to hear about your commitment to Christ and to celebrate with you! I want you to share your story with me. Write me a letter or send an e-mail and tell me when you made this decision to follow Christ and share with me the circumstances of this outstanding event. I will be praying for you that God will keep you and protect you in His great love.

Perry Stone, Jr.
PO BOX 3595
CLEVELAND, TN 37320-3595
E-Mail: *PerryStone@voe.org*

"You shall not be afraid of the terror by night, nor of the arrow that flies by day" (Psalm 91:5).

Endnotes

Steven Runciman. *A History of the Crusades: Volume 1, The First Crusade and the Foundation of the Kingdom of Jerusalem*. Cambridge: 1987.

Ronald Reagan. *An American Life: The Autobiography*. Simon & Schuster, 1990.

http://sron.ruu.nl/~jheise/akkadian/mesopotamia.html. (Accessed 4/19/2006).

http://sron.ruu.nl/~jheise/akkadian/index.html. (Accessed 4/19/2006).

http://members.aol.com/bjw1106/marian99.htm (Accessed 4/18/2006)

http://www.christianitytoday.com/history/newsletter/2003/nov7.html (Accessed 4/26/2006).

http://www.culturewars.com/2004/DaVinci.html (Accessed 10/26/2006).

http://www.ewtn.com/fatima/apparitions/Third_Secret/Fatima.ht #3rd. (Accessed 4/28/2006).

http://www.fatima.org/thirdsecret/ratzinger.asp (Accessed 4/22/06).

Dan Brown. *The Da Vinci Code*. Doubleday: 2003.

Howard Taylor, Mary G. Taylor. *Hudson Taylor's Spiritual Secret*. Moody Press: 2004.

http://www.leaderu.com/popculture/dismantlingdavinci.html (Accessed 10/26/2006)

David Van Biema. "Mary Magdalene, Saint or Sinner?" *TIME*, August 11, 2003.

http://www.catholic-pages.com/grabbag/malachy.asp (Accessed 4/21/06).

http://www.newadvent.org/cathen/09565a.htm (Accessed 5/2/2006).

Michael Brown, *The Final Hour*. Faith: 1992.

Bart D. Ehrman. *Truth and Fiction in The Da Vinci Code: A Historian Reveals What We Really Know about Jesus, Mary Magdalene, and Constantine*. Oxford: 2004.

http://en.wikipedia.org/wiki/Our_Lady_of_Fatima. (Accessed 5/2/2006).

Jim Tetlow, Roger Oakland, Brad Myers. *Queen of Rome, Queen of Islam, Queen of All*. Eternal Productions: 2006.

http://www.womensenews.org/article.cfm?aid=2748 (Accessed 10/26/2006).

You Have Just Read Book 4...
Do You Have Books 1, 2, and 3?

Book 1
(paperback, 94 pages)

Item: BK-PBF
Price: $10

Plus shipping & handling

Book 2
(paperback, 126 pages)

Item: BK-PBF2
Price: $10

Plus shipping & handling

Book 3
(paperback, 163 pages)

Item: BK-PBF3
Price: $14

Plus shipping & handling

For Credit Card orders call 423.478.3456

For additional resource materials, or to order online, please visit **www.perrystone.org**

MasterCard VISA

(U.S. FUNDS ONLY)